TOGAF® 9 Foundation
Study Guide 4th Edition

CW01023125

The Open Group Publications available from Van Haren Publishing

The TOGAF Series:
The TOGAF® Standard, Version 9.2
The TOGAF® Standard, Version 9.2 – A Pocket Guide
TOGAF® 9 Foundation Study Guide, 4th Edition
TOGAF® 9 Certified Study Guide, 4th Edition

The Open Group Series:
The IT4IT™ Reference Architecture, Version 2.1
IT4IT™ for Managing the Business of IT – A Management Guide
IT4IT™ Foundation Study Guide, 2nd edition
The IT4IT™ Reference Architecture, Version 2.1 – A Pocket Guide
Cloud Computing for Business – The Open Group Guide
ArchiMate® 3.0.1 – A Pocket Guide
ArchiMate® 2 Certification – Study Guide
ArchiMate® 3.0.1 Specification

The Open Group Security Series:
O-TTPS - A Management Guide
Open Information Security Management Maturity Model (O-ISM3)
Open Enterprise Security Architecture (O-ESA)
Risk Management – The Open Group Guide
The Open FAIR™ Body of Knowledge – A Pocket Guide

All titles are available to purchase from:
www.opengroup.org
www.vanharen.net
and also many international and online distributors.

TOGAF® 9 Foundation

Study Guide

4th Edition

Preparation for the TOGAF 9 Part 1 Examination

Prepared by Rachel Harrison of Oxford Brookes University and
Andrew Josey, The Open Group

Title:	TOGAF® Version 9 Foundation Study Guide 4th Edition
Subtitle:	Preparation for the TOGAF 9 Part 1 Examination
Series:	TOGAF Series
A Publication of:	The Open Group
Author:	Prof. Rachel Harrison and Andrew Josey
Publisher:	Van Haren Publishing, Zaltbommel, www.vanharen.net
ISBN Hard copy:	978 94 018 0289 5
ISBN eBook (pdf)	978 94 018 0290 1
ISBN ePUB:	978 94 018 0291 8
Edition:	Fourth edition, first impression, April 2018
Layout and Cover design:	Coco Bookmedia, Amersfoort –NL
Print:	Wilco, Amersfoort – NL

Study Guide
TOGAF® 9 Foundation, 4th Edition
Document Number: B180

Published by The Open Group, April 2018.

Comments relating to the material contained in this document may be submitted to:
The Open Group
Apex Plaza
Reading
Berkshire, RG1 1AX
United Kingdom
or by electronic mail to:
ogspecs@opengroup.org

Contents

Preface

This Document

This document is a Study Guide for the TOGAF® 9 Foundation qualification. This fourth edition is based on Version 3 of The Open Group Certification for People: Conformance Requirements (Multi-Level), and is aligned with the TOGAF Standard, Version 9.2.

It gives an overview of every learning objective for the TOGAF 9 Foundation Syllabus and in-depth coverage on preparing and taking the TOGAF 9 Part 1 Examination. It is specifically designed to help individuals prepare for certification.

The audience for this Study Guide is:
- Individuals who require a basic understanding of the TOGAF 9 framework
- Professionals who are working in roles associated with an architecture project such as those responsible for planning, execution, development, delivery, and operation
- Architects who are looking for a first introduction to the TOGAF 9 framework
- Architects who want to achieve Level 2 certification in a stepwise manner

A prior knowledge of Enterprise Architecture is advantageous but not required. While reading this Study Guide, the reader should also refer to the TOGAF 9 standard.[1]

The Study Guide is structured as shown below. The order of topics corresponds to the learning units of the TOGAF 9 Foundation Syllabus (see Appendix D).
- Chapter 1 (Introduction) provides a brief introduction to TOGAF certification and the TOGAF 9 Part 1 Examination that leads to TOGAF 9 Foundation, as well as how to use this Study Guide

---

[1] The TOGAF Standard, Version 9.2 (C182), available at www.opengroup.org/library/c182.

- Chapter 2 (Basic Concepts) introduces the basic concepts of Enterprise Architecture and the TOGAF standard; this provides a high-level view of the TOGAF framework, Enterprise Architecture, architecture frameworks, the contents of the TOGAF standard, and the TOGAF Library
- Chapter 3 (Core Concepts) describes the core concepts of the TOGAF 9 framework
- Chapter 4 (Key Terminology) introduces the key terminology of the TOGAF 9 standard
- Chapter 5 (Introduction to the ADM) introduces the Architecture Development Method (ADM), the objectives of each phase of the ADM, and how to adapt and scope the ADM for use
- Chapter 6 (The Enterprise Continuum and Tools) describes the Enterprise Continuum and tools; its purpose, and its constituent parts
- Chapter 7 (The ADM Phases) describes how each of the ADM phases contributes to the success of Enterprise Architecture
- Chapter 8 (ADM Guidelines and Techniques) describes guidelines and techniques provided to support application of the ADM
- Chapter 9 (Architecture Governance) describes Architecture Governance
- Chapter 10 (Views, Viewpoints, and Stakeholders) introduces the concepts of views and viewpoints and their role in communicating with stakeholders
- Chapter 11 (Building Blocks) introduces the concept of building blocks
- Chapter 12 (ADM Deliverables) describes the key deliverables of the ADM cycle and their purpose
- Chapter 13 (TOGAF Reference Models) describes the TOGAF reference models from the TOGAF Library: the Technical Reference Model (TRM) and the Integrated Information Infrastructure Reference Model (III-RM)
- Appendix A (Answers to Test Yourself Questions) provides the answers to the Test Yourself sections provided at the end of each chapter
- Appendix B (Test Yourself Examination Papers) provides two Test Yourself examinations to allow you to assess your knowledge of the TOGAF 9 Foundation Syllabus and readiness to take the TOGAF 9 Part 1 Examination
- Appendix C (Test Yourself Examination Paper Answers) provides the answers to the examinations in Appendix B
- Appendix D (TOGAF 9 Foundation Syllabus) provides the TOGAF 9 Foundation Syllabus

How to Use this Study Guide

The chapters in this Study Guide are arranged to follow the organization of the TOGAF 9 Foundation Syllabus (see Appendix D) and should be read in order. However, you may wish to use this Study Guide during review of topics with which you are already familiar, and it is possible to select topics for review in any order. Where a topic requires further information from a later part in the syllabus, a cross-reference is provided.

Within each chapter are "Key Learning Points" and "Summary" sections that help you to easily identify what you need to know for each topic.

Each chapter has a "Test Yourself" questions section that will help you to test your understanding of the chapter and prepare for the TOGAF 9 Part 1 Examination. The purpose of this is to reinforce key learning points in the chapter. These are multiple-choice format questions where you must identify one correct answer.

Each chapter also has a "Recommended Reading" section that indicates the relevant sections in the TOGAF 9 documentation that can be read to obtain a further understanding of the subject material.

Finally, at the end of this Study Guide are two "Test Yourself" examination papers that you can use to test your readiness to take the official TOGAF 9 Part 1 Examination. These papers are designed to include the same question formats and a similar difficulty level to the official TOGAF 9 Part 1 Examination.

Conventions Used in this Study Guide

The following conventions are used throughout this Study Guide in order to help identify important information and avoid confusion over the intended meaning.

- Ellipsis (…)
  Indicates a continuation; such as an incomplete list of example items, or a continuation from preceding text.
- **Bold**
  Used to highlight specific terms.
- *Italics*
  Used for emphasis. May also refer to other external documents.

- (Syllabus reference: Unit X, Learning Outcome Y: Statement)
  Used at the start of a text block to identify the TOGAF 9 Foundation
  Syllabus learning outcome.

In addition to typographical conventions, the following conventions are used
to highlight segments of text:

A Note box is used to highlight useful or interesting information.

A Tip box is used to provide key information that can save you time or that may not
be entirely obvious.

About the TOGAF Standard

The TOGAF Standard, a standard of The Open Group, is a proven Enterprise
Architecture methodology and framework used by the world's leading
organizations to improve business efficiency. It is the most prominent and
reliable Enterprise Architecture standard, ensuring consistent standards,
methods, and communication among Enterprise Architecture professionals.
Those fluent in the TOGAF standard enjoy greater industry credibility,
job effectiveness, and career opportunities. The TOGAF standard helps
practitioners avoid being locked into proprietary methods, utilize resources
more efficiently and effectively, and realize a greater return on investment.

About The Open Group

The Open Group is a global consortium that enables the achievement of
business objectives through technology standards. Our diverse membership
of more than 580 organizations includes customers, systems and solutions
suppliers, tools vendors, integrators, academics, and consultants across
multiple industries.

The Open Group aims to:

- Capture, understand, and address current and emerging requirements,
  establish policies, and share best practices

- Facilitate interoperability, develop consensus, and evolve and integrate specifications and open source technologies
- Operate the industry's premier certification service

Further information on The Open Group is available at www.opengroup.org.

The Open Group publishes a wide range of technical documentation, most of which is focused on development of Open Group Standards and Guides, but which also includes white papers, technical studies, certification and testing documentation, and business titles. Full details and a catalog are available at www.opengroup.org/library.

About the Authors

Rachel Harrison, Oxford Brookes University
Rachel Harrison is a Professor of Computer Science in the Department
of Computing and Communication Technologies at Oxford Brookes
University. Previously she was Professor of Computer Science, Head of the
Department of Computer Science, and Director of Research for the School
of Systems Engineering at the University of Reading. Her research interests
include systems evolution, software metrics, requirements engineering,
software architecture, usability, and software testing. She has published
over 100 refereed papers and consulted widely with industry, working with
organizations such as IBM, the DERA, Philips Research Labs, Praxis Critical
Systems, and The Open Group. She is Editor-in-Chief of the Software Quality
Journal, published by Springer.

Prof. Harrison holds an MA in Mathematics from Oxford University, an
MSc in Computer Science from University College London, and a PhD in
Computer Science from the University of Southampton. She is a Member of
the British Computer Society, an Affiliate Member of the IEEE-CS, a Member
of the Association of Computing Machinery, and is a Chartered Engineer.

Andrew Josey, The Open Group
Andrew Josey is VP Standards and Certification, overseeing all certification
and testing programs of The Open Group. He also manages the standards
process for The Open Group. Since joining the company in 1996, Andrew
has been closely involved with the standards development, certification,
and testing activities of The Open Group. He has led many standards
development projects including specification and certification development
for the ArchiMate®, TOGAF®, POSIX®, and UNIX® programs.

He is a member of the IEEE, USENIX, and the Association of Enterprise
Architects (AEA). He holds an MSc in Computer Science from University
College London.

Trademarks

Acknowledgements

The Open Group gratefully acknowledges The Open Group Architecture Forum for developing the TOGAF standard.

The Open Group gratefully acknowledges the following reviewers who participated in the review of this and earlier editions of this Study Guide:

- Corinne Brouch
- Geoff Burke
- Steve Else
- Bill Estrem
- Cathy Fox
- Kyle Gabhart
- Howard Gottlieb
- Paul Holdforth
- Henk Jonkers
- Andrew Josey
- Graham Neal
- Kiichiro Onishi
- Arnold van Overeem
- Andras Szakal
- Robert Weisman
- Ron Widitz

References

The following documents are referenced in this Study Guide:

- Analysis Patterns – Reusable Object Models, M. Fowler, Addison-Wesley
- Bill Estrem: "TOGAF to the Rescue" (www.opengroup.org/downloads)
- EU Directives on the Award of Public Contracts
- Interoperable Enterprise Business Scenario, October 2002 (K022), published by The Open Group; refer to: www.opengroup.org/library/k022
- ISO/IEC/IEEE 15288:2015, Systems and Software Engineering – System Life Cycle Processes
- ISO/IEC/IEEE 42010:2011, Systems and Software Engineering – Architecture Description
- The Clinger-Cohen Act (US Information Technology Management Reform Act 1996)
- The Open Group Certification for People: Certification Policy for Examination-Based Programs, April 2016 (X1603), published by The Open Group; refer to: www.opengroup.org/library/x1603
- The Open Group Certification for People: Program Summary Datasheet, 2018, published by The Open Group (www.opengroup.org/togaf9/cert/docs/togaf9_cert_summary.pdf)
- The Open Group Certification for People: TOGAF® Conformance Requirements (Multi-Level), Version 3.0, April 2018 (X1810), published by The Open Group; refer to: www.opengroup.org/library/x1810
- The Sarbanes-Oxley Act (US Public Company Accounting Reform and Investor Protection Act 2002)
- The TOGAF® Standard, Version 9.2, a standard of The Open Group, April 2018 (C182), published by The Open Group; refer to: www.opengroup.org/library/x1810
- TOGAF® 9 Foundation Datasheet, 2018, published by The Open Group (www.opengroup.org/togaf9/cert/docs/togaf9_foundation.pdf)
- TOGAF® Series Guide: Business Scenarios, September 2017 (G176), published by The Open Group; refer to www.opengroup.org/library/g176
- TOGAF® Series Guide: The TOGAF Integrated Information Infrastructure Reference Model (III- RM): An Architected Approach to Boundaryless Information Flow™, November 2017 (G179), published by The Open Group; refer to www.opengroup.org/library/g179

- TOGAF® Series Guide: The TOGAF Technical Reference Model (TRM), September 2017 (G175), published by The Open Group; refer to www.opengroup.org/library/g175
- Why Does Enterprise Architecture Matter?, White Paper by Simon Townson, SAP, November 2008 (W076), published by The Open Group; refer to: www.opengroup.org/library/w076

The following web links are referenced in this Study Guide:
- The Open Group TOGAF 9 Certification website: www.opengroup.org/certifications/togaf
- The TOGAF information website: www.togaf.info

Chapter 1

Introduction

1.1 Key Learning Points

This document is a Study Guide for students planning to become certified for TOGAF 9 Foundation. This edition is aligned to the approved syllabus for the TOGAF Standard, Version 9.2. It will familiarize you with all the topics that you need to know in order to pass the TOGAF 9 Part 1 Examination.

It gives an overview of every learning objective for the TOGAF 9 Foundation Syllabus and in-depth coverage on preparing and taking the TOGAF 9 Part 1 Examination. It is specifically designed to help individuals prepare for certification.

This first chapter will familiarize you with the TOGAF 9 certification program and its principles, as well as give you important information about the structure of the TOGAF 9 Part 1 Examination.

The objectives of this chapter are as follows:
- To provide an understanding of TOGAF certification and why you should become certified
- To learn key facts about the TOGAF 9 Part 1 Examination

1.2 The Open Group Certification for People Program

(Syllabus Reference: Unit 13, Learning Outcome 1: You should be able to briefly explain the TOGAF certification program, and distinguish between the levels for certification.)

Certification is available to individuals who wish to demonstrate they have attained the required knowledge and understanding of the TOGAF Standard, Version 9.[2]

---

2   This edition of this Study Guide covers Version 3 of The Open Group Certification for People: TOGAF Conformance Requirements (Multi-Level), which are aligned to the TOGAF Standard, Version 9.2.

There are two levels defined for TOGAF 9 People certification, denoted Level 1 and Level 2, which lead to certification at TOGAF 9 Foundation and TOGAF 9 Certified, respectively. This Study Guide covers the first of these – TOGAF 9 Foundation. Studying for TOGAF 9 Foundation can be used as a learning objective towards achieving TOGAF 9 Certified, as the learning outcomes in TOGAF 9 Foundation are also required in TOGAF 9 Certified.

Table 1:   Certification Levels and Associated Labels

Certification Level	Certification Label
Level 1	TOGAF 9 Foundation
Level 2	TOGAF 9 Certified

Why is TOGAF certification important?

The existence of a certification program for the TOGAF standard provides a strong incentive for organizations to standardize on the TOGAF standard as the open method for Enterprise Architecture, and so avoid lock-in to proprietary methods. It is an important step in making Enterprise Architecture a well-recognized discipline, and in introducing rigor into the procurement of tools and services for Enterprise Architecture.

The two certification levels are summarized in Figure 1. Figure 1 shows the relationship between Level 1 and Level 2. Level 2 (TOGAF 9 Certified) is a superset of the requirements for Level 1 (TOGAF 9 Foundation).[3]

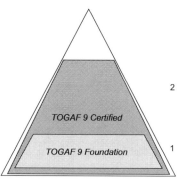

Figure 1:   TOGAF 9 Certification Program Overview

---

3   The gap at the top of the pyramid is to signify that additional credential-based certification is planned beyond Level 2.

1.2.1 Certification Document Structure

The documents available to support the Program are as shown in Figure 2.

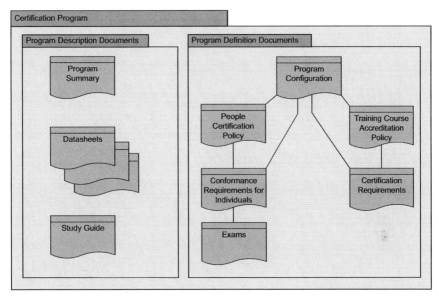

Figure 2:   Certification Document Structure

Program description documents, such as this Study Guide, are intended for an end-user audience including those interested in becoming certified. The Program definition documents are intended for trainers, examination developers, and the Certification Authority. All these documents are available from The Open Group website.[4]

Why become certified?

Becoming certified demonstrates clearly to employers and peers your commitment to Enterprise Architecture as a discipline. In particular, it demonstrates that you possess a body of core knowledge about the TOGAF standard as an open, industry standard framework and method for Enterprise Architecture. The Open Group publishes the definitive directory of TOGAF Certified individuals, and certified service and product offerings, and issues certificates.

---

4   Available from the TOGAF 9 Certification website at www.opengroup.org/certifications/togaf9, or from The Open Group Library at www.opengroup.org/library.

1.2.2 Program Vision and Principles

The vision for the Program is to define and promote a market-driven education and certification program to support the TOGAF 9 framework. The Open Group certification programs are designed with the following principles in mind:

Table 2:   The Open Group Certification Program Principles

Principle	Certification Aspects
Openness	Certification is open to applicants from all countries.[5]
Fairness	Certification is achieved only by passing an examination that is equivalent to that taken by any other candidate.
Market Relevance	Each Program is designed to meet the perceived needs of the market.
Learning Support	Training courses are provided by third parties, according to the needs of the market.
Quality	Training course providers may choose to seek accreditation from The Open Group for their courses. Accredited courses are listed on The Open Group website.
Best Practice	The Programs are designed to follow industry best practice for equivalent certification programs.

1.2.3 TOGAF 9 Foundation

The purpose of certification to TOGAF 9 Level 1, known as TOGAF 9 Foundation, is to provide validation that the candidate has gained an acceptable level of knowledge of the TOGAF terminology, structure, and basic concepts, and understands the core principles of Enterprise Architecture and the TOGAF standard.

The learning objectives at this level focus on knowledge and comprehension. Individuals certified at this level will have demonstrated their understanding of:

- The basic concepts of Enterprise Architecture and the TOGAF framework

---

5   Subject to compliance with applicable United States laws, regulations, or orders including those relating to export including but not limited to International Traffic in Arms Regulations (ITAR) and/or Export Administration Act/Regulations (EAR).

- The core concepts of the TOGAF standard
- The key terminology of the TOGAF standard
- The ADM cycle and the objectives of each phase, and how to adapt and scope the ADM
- The concept of the Enterprise Continuum; its purpose, and its constituent parts
- How each of the ADM phases contributes to the success of Enterprise Architecture
- The ADM guidelines and techniques
- How Architecture Governance contributes to the Architecture Development Cycle
- The concepts of views and viewpoints and their role in communicating with stakeholders
- The concept of building blocks
- The key deliverables of the ADM cycle
- The two example TOGAF reference models
- The TOGAF certification program

Examination

Certification for TOGAF 9 Foundation is achieved by passing the TOGAF 9 Part 1 Examination. This is a multiple-choice examination with 40 questions.[6]

What is the relationship between TOGAF 9 Foundation and TOGAF 9 Certified?
The learning outcomes for TOGAF 9 Foundation are a subset of those for TOGAF 9 Certified. Candidates are able to choose whether they wish to become certified in a stepwise manner by starting with TOGAF 9 Foundation and then at a later date TOGAF 9 Certified, or alternately to go direct to TOGAF 9 Certified by taking the combined examination.

1.2.4 The Certification Process

This Study Guide is aimed at preparing you to become certified for TOGAF 9 Foundation.

The TOGAF 9 Foundation Syllabus for the examination is contained in

---

6 For the latest information on examinations, see the TOGAF 9 Certification website at www.opengroup.org/certifications/togaf9.

Appendix D. Certain topic areas are weighted as more important than others and thus have more questions. The 11 topic areas covered by the examination together with the number of questions per area in the examination follow:

1. Basic Concepts (3 questions)
2. Core Concepts (3 questions)
3. Introduction to the ADM (3 questions)
4. The Enterprise Continuum and Tools (4 questions)
5. ADM Phases (9 questions)
6. ADM Guidelines and Techniques (6 questions)
7. Architecture Governance (4 questions)
8. Architecture Views, Viewpoints, and Stakeholders (2 questions)
9. Building Blocks (2 questions)
10. ADM Deliverables (2 questions)
11. TOGAF Reference Models (2 questions)

1.2.4.1 Format of the Examination Questions
The examination questions are multiple-choice questions. These are very similar in format to the Test Yourself questions included in each chapter. Note that the exact format for display is test center-specific and will be made clear on the screens when taking the examination.

Exam Tip
Please read each question carefully before reading the answer options. Be aware that some questions may seem to have more than one right answer, but you are to look for the one that makes the most sense and is the most correct.

1.2.4.2 What do I need to bring with me to take the Examination?
You should consult with the exam provider regarding the forms of picture ID you are required to bring with you to verify your identification.

1.2.4.3 Can I refer to materials while I take the Examination?
No; it is a closed-book examination.

1.2.4.4 If I fail, how soon can I retake the Examination?
You should check the current policy on The Open Group website. At the time of writing, the policy states that individuals who have failed the examination are not allowed to retake the examination within one (1) month of the first sitting.

1.2.5 Preparing for the Examination

You can prepare for the examination by working through this Study Guide section-by-section. A mapping of the sections of this Study Guide to the TOGAF 9 Foundation Syllabus is given in Appendix D. After completing each section, you should answer the Test Yourself questions and read the referenced sections from the TOGAF documentation. Once you have completed all the sections in this Study Guide, you can then attempt the Test Yourself examination papers in Appendix B. These are designed to give a thorough test of your knowledge. If you have completed all the prescribed preparation and can attain a pass mark for the Test Yourself examination papers as described in Appendix C, then it is likely you are ready to sit the examination.

1.3 Summary

The Open Group Certification for People: TOGAF Certification Program is a knowledge-based certification program. It has two levels, Level 1 and Level 2, which lead to certification for TOGAF 9 Foundation and TOGAF 9 Certified, respectively.

The topic for this Study Guide is preparation for taking the TOGAF 9 Part 1 Examination that leads to the TOGAF 9 Foundation certification. The examination comprises 40 simple multiple-choice questions to be completed in one hour.[7]

Preparing for the examination includes the following steps:
- You should work through this Study Guide step-by-step
- At the end of each chapter, you should complete the Test Yourself questions and read the sections of the TOGAF documentation listed under Recommended Reading

---

7   Additional time is allowed for candidates for whom English is a second language where the examination is not available in the local language. For further information see the advice to candidates sheet on The Open Group TOGAF 9 Certification website.

- Once you have completed all the chapters in this Study Guide, you should attempt the Test Yourself examination papers given in Appendix B
- If you can attain the target score in Appendix C, then you have completed your preparation

1.4 Test Yourself Questions

Q1:   Which of the following describes the TOGAF 9 Part 1 Examination?
   A.   It is an open book examination
   A.   It has 40 simple multiple-choice questions
   B.   The exam policy requires you to wait 60 days before a retake
   C.   It contains at least four questions related to building blocks

Q2:   Which one of the following is the entry-level certification for an individual?
   A.   TOGAF 9 Certified
   B.   TOGAF 9 Foundation
   C.   TOGAF 9 Professional
   D.   TOGAF 9 Architect

Q3:   Which one of the following describes three principles of The Open Group Certification for People: TOGAF Certification Program?
   A.   Integrity, Scalability, Flexibility
   B.   Objectivity, Robustness, Simplicity
   C.   Openness, Fairness, Quality
   D.   Knowledge-based, Valuable, Simplicity
   E.   All of these

Q4:   Which of the following topic areas is *not* included in the TOGAF 9 Foundation Syllabus?
   A.   Architecture Governance
   B.   Basic Concepts
   C.   Building Blocks
   D.   Guidelines for adapting the ADM: Iteration and Levels
   E.   Introduction to the ADM

1.5 Recommended Reading

The following are recommended sources of further information for this chapter:

- The Open Group Certification for People: Program Summary Datasheet
- TOGAF 9 Foundation Datasheet
- The Open Group Certification for People: Certification Policy for Examination-Based Programs
- The Open Group Certification for People: TOGAF Conformance Requirements (Multi-Level)
- The Open Group TOGAF 9 Certification website: www.opengroup.org/certifications/togaf9
- The TOGAF information website: www.togaf.info

Chapter 2

Basic Concepts

2.1 Key Learning Points

This chapter will familiarize you with the fundamentals that you need to know to pass the TOGAF 9 Part 1 Examination. The objectives of this chapter are as follows:

- To provide an introduction to the basic concepts of Enterprise Architecture and the TOGAF framework, including providing a high-level view of the TOGAF standard, Enterprise Architecture, architecture frameworks, and the contents of the TOGAF 9 standard

Key Points Explained

This chapter will help you to answer the following questions:

- What is the TOGAF standard?
- What is an enterprise?
- What is Enterprise Architecture?
- Why do I need Enterprise Architecture? What are the business benefits?
- What is "architecture" in the context of the TOGAF standard?
- What is an architecture framework?
- Why do I need a framework for Enterprise Architecture?
- Why is the TOGAF standard suitable as a framework for Enterprise Architecture?
- What does the TOGAF standard contain?
- What are the different types of architecture that the TOGAF standard deals with?

2.2 Introduction to the TOGAF 9 Standard

2.2.1 What is the TOGAF Standard?

(Syllabus Reference: Unit 1, Learning Outcome 7: You should be able to briefly explain what the TOGAF standard is.)

The TOGAF standard is an architecture framework. It provides the methods and tools for assisting in the acceptance, production, use, and maintenance of

Enterprise Architectures. It is based on an iterative process model supported by best practices and a re-usable set of existing architectural assets.

The TOGAF standard is developed and maintained by The Open Group Architecture Forum. The first version of the TOGAF standard, developed in 1995, was based on the US Department of Defense Technical Architecture Framework for Information Management (TAFIM). Starting from this sound foundation, The Open Group Architecture Forum has developed successive versions of the TOGAF standard at regular intervals and published each one on The Open Group public website.

The TOGAF standard can be used for developing a broad range of different Enterprise Architectures. It complements, and can be used in conjunction with, other frameworks that are more focused on specific deliverables for particular vertical sectors such as Government, Telecommunications, Manufacturing, Defense, and Finance. A key part of the TOGAF standard is the method – the TOGAF Architecture Development Method (ADM) – for developing an Enterprise Architecture that addresses business needs.

Study Guide References

When appropriate, this Study Guide contains references to sections within the TOGAF Standard, Version 9.2 and relevant documents from the TOGAF Library. The references are intended to be functional for the web version and printed version of the document. Therefore, the format of the reference number contains both the Part and the Chapter reference, but not the page references since they exist only in the printed book.

2.2.2 Structure of the TOGAF Documentation

(Syllabus Reference: Unit 1, Learning Outcome 6: You should be able to describe the structure of the TOGAF standard, and briefly explain the contents of each of the parts.)

The TOGAF documentation consists of the TOGAF standard, and a portfolio of guidance material, known as the TOGAF Library, to support the practical application of the standard.

Table 3 summarizes the parts of the TOGAF standard.

Table 3:   Structure of the TOGAF Standard

TOGAF Part	Summary
Part I: Introduction	This part provides a high-level introduction to the key concepts of Enterprise Architecture and, in particular, to the TOGAF approach. It contains the definitions of terms used throughout the standard.
Part II: Architecture Development Method (ADM)	This part is the core of the TOGAF framework. It describes the TOGAF Architecture Development Method (ADM) – a step-by-step approach to developing an Enterprise Architecture.
Part III: ADM Guidelines and Techniques	This part contains a collection of guidelines and techniques available for use in applying the TOGAF approach and the TOGAF ADM. (Additional guidelines and techniques are also in the TOGAF Library.)
Part IV: Architecture Content Framework	This part describes the TOGAF content framework, including a structured metamodel for architectural artifacts, the use of re-usable Architecture Building Blocks (ABBs), and an overview of typical architecture deliverables.
Part V: Enterprise Continuum and Tools	This part discusses appropriate taxonomies and tools to categorize and store the outputs of architecture activity within an enterprise.
Part VI: Architecture Capability Framework	This part discusses the organization, processes, skills, roles, and responsibilities required to establish and operate an architecture practice within an enterprise.

(Syllabus Reference: Unit 1, Learning Outcome 10: You should be able to briefly explain the TOGAF Library.)

Accompanying the standard is the TOGAF Library. The TOGAF Library is a reference library containing guidelines, templates, patterns, and other forms of reference material to accelerate the creation of new architectures for the enterprise. It is structured as summarized in Table 4:

Table 4:   Structure of the TOGAF Library

Section 1: Foundation Documents	Broadly applicable information relating to the subject of the TOGAF framework or Enterprise Architecture.
Section 2: Generic Guidance and Techniques	Information describing architecture styles and how the TOGAF framework and Enterprise Architecture can be adapted to exploit the characteristics of a more specific context.
Section 3: Industry-Specific Guidance and Techniques	Information describing how the TOGAF framework and Enterprise Architecture can be applied to meet the specific needs of a vertical industry segment.
Section 4: Organization-Specific Guidance and Techniques	Information describing how the TOGAF framework and Enterprise Architecture have been applied to meet the needs of specific enterprises.

2.3 What is an Enterprise?

(Syllabus Reference: Unit 1, Learning Outcome 1: You should be able describe what an enterprise is.)

The TOGAF standard considers an "enterprise" to be any collection of organizations that has common goals. For example, an enterprise could be a whole corporation, or a division of a corporation; a government agency or a single government department; a chain of geographically distant organizations linked together by common ownership; groups of countries or governments working together to create common or shareable deliverables or infrastructures; partnerships and alliances of businesses working together, such as a consortium or supply chain.

The term "enterprise" in the context of "Enterprise Architecture" can be used to denote both an entire enterprise, encompassing all of its information systems, and a specific domain within the enterprise. In both cases, the architecture crosses multiple systems and multiple functional groups within the enterprise.

Confusion often arises from the evolving nature of the term "enterprise". An extended enterprise frequently includes partners, suppliers, and customers. If the goal is to integrate an extended enterprise, then the enterprise comprises the partners, suppliers, and customers, as well as internal business units.

For example, an organization with an online store that uses an external fulfillment house for dispatching orders would extend its definition of the enterprise in that system to include the fulfillment house.

2.4 What is Architecture in the Context of the TOGAF Standard?

(Syllabus Reference: Unit 1, Learning Outcome 8: You should be able to explain what architecture is in the context of the TOGAF standard.)

ISO/IEC/IEEE 42010:2011[8] defines "architecture" as:

"The fundamental concepts or properties of a system in its environment embodied in its elements, relationships, and in the principles of its design and evolution."

The TOGAF standard embraces but does not strictly adhere to ISO/IEC/IEEE 42010:2011 terminology. In addition to the ISO/IEC/IEEE 42010:2011 definition, the TOGAF standard adds a second definition depending on the context:

"The structure of components, their inter-relationships, and the principles and guidelines governing their design and evolution over time."

---

8   ISO/IEC/IEEE 42010: 2011, Systems and Software Engineering — Architecture Description.

What is Enterprise Architecture?

There are many definitions of Enterprise Architecture. Most focus on structure and organization. Two definitions are given below:

Enterprise Architecture is:

1. The organizing logic for business processes and IT infrastructure reflecting the integration and standardization requirements of the firm's operating model. [Source: MIT Center for Information Systems Research]

2. A conceptual blueprint that defines the structure and operation of an organization. The intent of an Enterprise Architecture is to determine how an organization can most effectively achieve its current and future objectives. [Source: SearchCIO.com]

2.5 Why do I Need Enterprise Architecture?

(Syllabus Reference: Unit 1, Learning Outcome 2: You should be able to explain the purpose of an Enterprise Architecture.)

The purpose of Enterprise Architecture is to optimize across the enterprise the often fragmented legacy of processes (both manual and automated) into an integrated environment that is responsive to change and supportive of the delivery of the business strategy. Effective management and exploitation of information and Digital Transformation are key factors to business success, and an indispensable means to achieving competitive advantage. An Enterprise Architecture addresses this need, by providing a strategic context for the evolution and reach of digital capability in response to the constantly changing needs of the business environment.

For example, the rapid development of social media, Internet of Things, and cloud computing has radically extended the capacity of the enterprise to create new market opportunities.

(Syllabus Reference: Unit 1, Learning Outcome 3: You should be able to list the business benefits of having an Enterprise Architecture.)

The advantages that result from a good Enterprise Architecture can bring important business benefits, including:

- More effective and efficient business operations:
    - Lower business operation costs

- — More agile organization
- — Business capabilities shared across the organization
- — Lower change management costs
- — More flexible workforce
- — Improved business productivity
- More effective and efficient Digital Transformation and IT operations:
  - — Extending the effective reach of the enterprise through digital capability
  - — Bringing all components of the enterprise into a harmonized environment
  - — Lower software development, support, and maintenance costs
  - — Increased portability of applications
  - — Improved interoperability and easier system and network management
  - — Improved ability to address critical enterprise-wide issues, such as security
  - — Easier upgrade and exchange of system components
- Better return on existing investment, reduced risk for future investment:
  - — Reduced complexity in the business and IT
  - — Maximum return on investment in existing business and IT infrastructure
  - — The flexibility to make, buy, or out-source business and IT solutions
  - — Reduced risk overall in new investments and their costs of ownership
- Faster, simpler, and cheaper procurement:
  - — Simpler buying decisions, because the information governing procurement is readily available in a coherent plan
  - — Faster procurement process, maximizing procurement speed and flexibility without sacrificing architectural coherence
  - — The ability to procure heterogeneous, multi-vendor open systems
  - — The ability to secure more economic capabilities

Ultimately, the benefits of Enterprise Architecture derive from the better planning, earlier visibility, and more informed designs that result when it is introduced.
[Source: Simon Townson, Why Does Enterprise Architecture Matter?]

2.6 What is an Architecture Framework?

(Syllabus Reference: Unit 1, Learning Outcome 4: You should be able to define what an architecture framework is.)

An architecture framework is a foundational structure, or set of structures, that can be used for developing a broad range of different architectures. It should describe a method for designing a target state of the enterprise in terms of a set of building blocks, and for showing how the building blocks fit together. It should contain a set of tools and provide a common vocabulary. It should also include a list of recommended standards and compliant products that can be used to implement the building blocks.

2.7 Why do I Need a Framework for Enterprise Architecture?

Using an architecture framework will speed up and simplify architecture development, ensure more complete coverage of the designed solution, and make certain that the architecture selected allows for future growth in response to the needs of the business.

Regulatory Drivers for Adoption of Enterprise Architecture

There are a number of laws and regulations that have been drivers for the adoption and use of Enterprise Architecture in business:

- The Clinger-Cohen Act

  (US Information Technology Management Reform Act 1996)

  The US Information Technology Management Reform Act (Clinger-Cohen Act) is designed to improve the way the US Federal Government acquires and manages IT.

- The Sarbanes-Oxley Act

  (US Public Company Accounting Reform and Investor Protection Act 2002)

  The Sarbanes-Oxley Act was passed in response to a number of major corporate and accounting scandals involving prominent companies in the US (for example, Enron and Worldcom). Under the Act, companies must provide attestation of internal control assessment, including documentation of control procedures related to IT.

- EU Directives on the Award of Public Contracts

  Similarly within the European Union, there are EU Directives that require vendors involved in Public Contracts to show that they are using formal Enterprise Architecture processes within their businesses when supplying products and services.

2.8 Why is the TOGAF Standard Suitable as a Framework for Enterprise Architecture?

(Syllabus Reference: Unit 1, Learning Outcome 5: You should be able explain why the TOGAF standard is suitable as a framework for Enterprise Architecture.)

The TOGAF standard has been developed through the collaborative efforts of the whole community. Using the TOGAF standard results in Enterprise Architecture that is consistent, reflects the needs of stakeholders, employs best practice, and gives due consideration both to current requirements and to the perceived future needs of the business.

Developing and sustaining an Enterprise Architecture is a technically complex process which involves many stakeholders and decision processes in the organization. The TOGAF standard plays an important role in standardizing and risk reduction of the architecture development process. The TOGAF standard provides a best practice framework for adding value, and enables the organization to build workable and economic solutions which address their business issues and needs.

2.9 What are the Different Architecture Domains that the TOGAF Standard deals with?

(Syllabus Reference: Unit 1, Learning Outcome 9: You should be able to list the different types of architecture that the TOGAF standard deals with.)

The TOGAF standard covers the development of four architecture domains. These are commonly accepted as subsets of an overall Enterprise Architecture. They are as follows:

Table 5:   Architecture Domains Supported by the TOGAF Standard

Architecture Type	Description
Business Architecture	The business strategy, governance, organization, and key business processes.
Data Architecture	The structure of an organization's logical and physical data assets and data management resources.
Application Architecture	A blueprint for the individual application systems to be deployed, their interactions, and their relationships to the core business processes of the organization.
Technology Architecture	The software and hardware capabilities that are required to support the deployment of business, data, and application services. This includes IT infrastructure, middleware, networks, communications, processing, and standards.

2.10 What does the TOGAF Standard Contain?

(Syllabus Reference: Unit 1, Learning Outcome 6: You should be able to describe the structure of the TOGAF standard, and briefly explain the contents of each of the parts.)

The contents of the TOGAF standard reflect the structure and content of an Architecture Capability within an enterprise, as shown in Figure 3.

Definition of "Capability"

An ability that an organization, person, or system possesses.

[Source: The TOGAF Standard, Version 9.2 Part I: Introduction, Chapter 3 (Definitions)]

Capabilities are typically expressed in general and high-level terms and typically require a combination of organization, people, processes, and technology to achieve. For example, marketing, customer contact, or outbound telemarketing.

An **Enterprise Architecture Capability** (or Architecture Capability), in the context of the TOGAF standard, is the ability for an organization to effectively undertake the activities of an Enterprise Architecture practice.

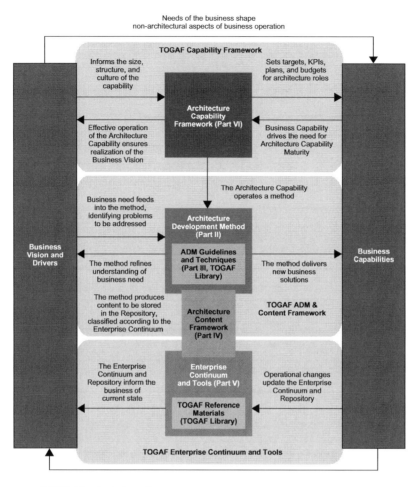

Figure 3:   TOGAF Content Overview

Central to the TOGAF framework is the Architecture Development Method
(documented in Part II: ADM). The Architecture Capability (documented
in Part VI: Architecture Capability Framework) operates the method. The
method is supported by a number of guidelines and techniques (documented
in Part III: ADM Guidelines and Techniques, and also in the TOGAF
Library). This produces content (documented in Part IV: Architecture
Content Framework) to be stored in the repository, which is classified
according to the Enterprise Continuum (documented in Part V: Enterprise
Continuum and Tools). The repository can be initially populated with the
TOGAF Reference Models and other reference materials (documented in the
TOGAF Library).

These are described in the following sections.

2.10.1 The Architecture Development Method (ADM)

The ADM describes a process for deriving an organization-specific Enterprise Architecture that addresses business requirements.

The ADM is the major component of the TOGAF framework and provides guidance for architects on a number of levels:

- It provides a number of **architecture development phases** (Business Architecture, Information Systems Architectures, Technology Architecture) in a cycle, as an overall process template for architecture development activity
- It provides a **narrative of each architecture phase**, describing the phase in terms of objectives, approach, inputs, steps, and outputs
  The inputs and outputs sections provide a definition of the architecture content structure and deliverables (a detailed description of the phase inputs and phase outputs is given in the Architecture Content Framework).
- It provides cross-phase summaries that cover requirements management

See also Chapter 5 and Chapter 7.

2.10.2 ADM Guidelines and Techniques

ADM Guidelines and Techniques provides a number of guidelines and techniques to support the application of the ADM. The guidelines include adapting the ADM to deal with a number of usage scenarios, including different process styles (e.g., the use of iteration) and applying the ADM across the Architecture Landscape. There is a high-level description of how to use the framework with different architectural styles, using SOA as an example. The techniques support specific tasks within the ADM (such as Capability-Based Planning, defining principles, gap analysis, migration planning, risk management, stakeholder management, etc.). Additional guidelines and techniques are also available in the TOGAF Library (e.g., guidance on the business scenarios technique). See also Chapter 8.

2.10.3 Architecture Content Framework

The **Architecture Content Framework** provides a detailed model of architectural work products, including deliverables, artifacts within deliverables, and the Architecture Building Blocks (ABBs) that deliverables represent.

The details of the Architecture Content Framework are out of scope for TOGAF 9 Foundation, and are covered instead in the Level 2 syllabus.

2.10.4 The Enterprise Continuum

The **Enterprise Continuum** provides a model for structuring a virtual repository and provides methods for classifying architecture and solution artifacts, showing how the different types of artifacts evolve, and how they can be leveraged and re-used. This is based on architectures and solutions (models, patterns, architecture descriptions, etc.) that exist within the enterprise and in the industry at large, and which the enterprise has collected for use in the development of its architectures.

See also Section 3.4 and Chapter 6.

2.10.5 TOGAF Reference Models

The TOGAF Library includes two example reference models (as well as other reference materials) for possible inclusion in an enterprise's own Enterprise Continuum.

Table 6: Reference Models Included in the Enterprise Continuum

Reference Model	Description
TOGAF Foundation Architecture Technical Reference Model	The TOGAF Technical Reference Model is an architecture of generic services and functions that provides a foundation on which specific architectures and Architecture Building Blocks (ABBs) can be built.
Integrated Information Infrastructure Reference Model (III-RM)	The Integrated Information Infrastructure Reference Model (III-RM) is based on the TOGAF Foundation Architecture, and is specifically aimed at helping the design of architectures that enable and support the vision of Boundaryless Information Flow.

See also Chapter 13.

2.10.6 The Architecture Capability Framework

The **Architecture Capability Framework** is a set of resources, guidelines, templates, background information, etc. provided to help the architect establish an architecture practice within an organization.

See also Section 3.6, Section 3.7, and Chapter 9.

2.11 Summary

This chapter has introduced the basic concepts of Enterprise Architecture and the TOGAF standard. This has included answering questions, such as:
- "What is an enterprise?"
  - A collection of organizations that share common goals, such as a government agency, part of a corporation, or a corporation in its entirety
  - Large corporations may comprise multiple enterprises
  - An "extended enterprise" can include partners, suppliers, and customers
- "What is an architecture?"
  - An architecture is defined as "the fundamental concepts or properties of a system in its environment embodied in its elements, relationships, and in the principles of its design and evolution"

The TOGAF standard is an architecture framework. It enables you to design, evaluate, and build the right architecture for your organization. An architecture framework is a "toolkit" that can be used for developing a broad range of different architectures.
- It should describe a method to design an information system in terms of a set of building blocks, and show how the building blocks fit together
- It should contain a set of tools and provide a common vocabulary
- It should also include a list of recommended standards and compliant products that can be used to implement the building blocks

The value of a framework is that it provides a practical starting point for an architecture project.

The components of the TOGAF Standard, Version 9.2 are as follows:
- Architecture Development Method (ADM)
- ADM Guidelines and Techniques
- The Architecture Content Framework
- The Enterprise Continuum and Tools
- The Architecture Capability Framework

The TOGAF Library is a reference library containing guidelines, templates, patterns, and other forms of reference material to accelerate the creation of new architectures for the enterprise.

2.12 Test Yourself Questions

Q1: Which one of the following statements best describes the TOGAF standard?
  A. The TOGAF standard is a tool for developing Technology Architectures only.
  B. The TOGAF standard is a framework and method for architecture development.
  C. The TOGAF standard is an architecture pattern.
  D. The TOGAF standard is a method for IT Governance.

Q2: Which one of the following best describes why you need a framework for Enterprise Architecture?
  A. Architecture design is complex.
  B. Using a framework can speed up the process.
  C. Using a framework ensures more complete coverage.
  D. A framework provides a set of tools and a common vocabulary.
  E. All of these.

Q3: Which of the following is *not* one of the main constituent parts of the TOGAF standard?
  A. The Architecture Development Method
  B. The Enterprise Continuum & Tools
  C. The TOGAF Technical Reference Model
  D. The TOGAF Architecture Capability Framework

Q4:   Which one of the types of architecture below is *not* commonly
      accepted as part of the Enterprise Architecture addressed by the
      TOGAF standard?
      A.   Business Architecture
      B.   Data Architecture
      C.   Application Architecture
      D.   Technology Architecture
      E.   Pattern Architecture

Q5:   Which part of the TOGAF document provides a number of
      architecture development phases, together with narratives for each
      phase?
      A.   Part I: Introduction
      B.   Part II: Architecture Development Method (ADM)
      C.   Part III: ADM Guidelines and Techniques
      D.   Part IV: Architecture Content Framework
      E.   Part V: Enterprise Continuum and Tools

2.13 Recommended Reading

The following are recommended sources of further information for this
chapter:

- The TOGAF Standard, Version 9.2 Part I: Introduction, Introduction and
  Core Concepts
- Why Does Enterprise Architecture Matter?, White Paper by Simon
  Townson

Chapter 3

Core Concepts

3.1 Key Learning Points

This chapter will help you understand and be able to explain the core concepts of the TOGAF standard.

Key Points Explained

This chapter will help you to answer the following questions:

- What are the ADM phase names and the purpose of each phase?
- What are deliverables, artifacts, and building blocks?
- What is the Enterprise Continuum?
- What is the Architecture Repository?
- How to establish and operate an Enterprise Architecture Capability?
- How to use the TOGAF framework with other frameworks?

3.2 What are the Phases of the ADM?

(Syllabus Reference: Unit 2, Learning Outcome 1: You should be able to explain the core concept of the ADM and the purpose of each phase at a high level.)

The Architecture Development Method (ADM) forms the core of the TOGAF standard and is a method for deriving organization-specific Enterprise Architecture. It is the result of contributions from many architecture practitioners.

The ADM provides a tested and repeatable process for developing architectures. The ADM includes establishing an architecture framework, developing architecture content, transitioning, and governing the realization of architectures. All of these activities are carried out within an iterative cycle of continuous architecture definition and realization that allows organizations to transform their enterprises in a controlled manner in response to business goals and opportunities.

The ADM is described as a number of phases within a process of change illustrated by an ADM cycle graphic (see following). Phases within the ADM are as follows:

The **Preliminary Phase** describes the preparation and initiation activities required to create an Architecture Capability, including the customization of the TOGAF framework, and the definition of Architecture Principles.

Phase A: Architecture Vision describes the initial phase of an Architecture Development Cycle. It includes information about defining the scope, identifying the stakeholders, creating the Architecture Vision, and obtaining approvals.

Phase B: Business Architecture describes the development of a Business Architecture to support an agreed Architecture Vision.

Phase C: Information Systems Architectures describes the development of Information Systems Architectures for an architecture project, including the development of Data and Application Architectures.

Phase D: Technology Architecture describes the development of the Technology Architecture for an architecture project.

Phase E: Opportunities and Solutions describes the process of identifying major implementation projects and grouping them into work packages that deliver the Target Architecture defined in the previous phases.

Phase F: Migration Planning describes the development of a detailed Implementation and Migration Plan that addresses how to move from the Baseline to the Target Architecture.

Phase G: Implementation Governance provides an architectural oversight of the implementation.

Phase H: Architecture Change Management establishes procedures for managing change to the new architecture.

Requirements Management examines the process of managing architecture requirements throughout the ADM.

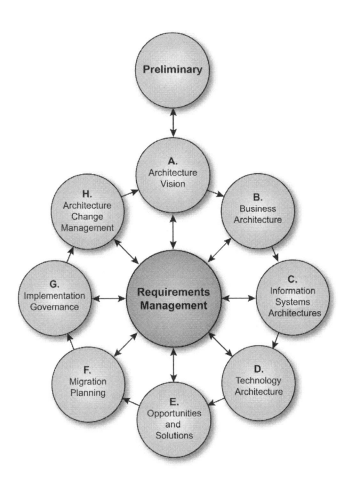

3.3 Deliverables, Artifacts, and Building Blocks

(Syllabus Reference: Unit 2, Learning Outcome 2: You should be able to explain the core concepts of deliverables, artifacts, and building blocks in the context of the Architecture Content Framework.)

During application of the ADM process, a number of outputs are produced; for example, process flows, architectural requirements, project plans, project compliance assessments, etc. In order to collate and present these major work products in a consistent and structured manner, the TOGAF standard defines a structural model – the TOGAF Architecture Content Framework – in which to place them.

The Architecture Content Framework uses the following three categories to describe the type of architectural work product within the context of use:

- A **deliverable** is a work product that is contractually specified and in turn formally reviewed, agreed, and signed off by the stakeholders
  Deliverables represent the output of projects and those deliverables that are in documentation form will typically be archived at completion of a project, or transitioned into an Architecture Repository as a reference model, standard, or snapshot of the Architecture Landscape at a point in time.
- An **artifact** is an architectural work product that describes an aspect of the architecture
  Artifacts are generally classified as catalogs (lists of things), matrices (showing relationships between things), and diagrams (pictures of things). Examples include a requirements catalog, business interaction matrix, and a use-case diagram. An architectural deliverable may contain many artifacts and artifacts will form the content of the Architecture Repository.
- A **building block** represents a (potentially re-usable) component of business, IT, or architectural capability that can be combined with other building blocks to deliver architectures and solutions
  Building blocks can be defined at various levels of detail and can relate to both architectures and solutions, with Architecture Building Blocks (ABBs) typically describing the required capability in order to shape the Solution Building Blocks (SBBs) which would represent the components to be used to implement the required capability.

The relationships between deliverables, artifacts, and building blocks are shown in Figure 4.

Figure 4: Relationships between Deliverables, Artifacts, and Building Blocks

3.4 The Enterprise Continuum

(Syllabus Reference: Unit 2, Learning Outcome 3: You should be able to explain the core concept of the Enterprise Continuum.)

The TOGAF standard includes the concept of the Enterprise Continuum, shown in Figure 5, which sets the broader context for an architect and explains how generic solutions can be leveraged and specialized in order to support the requirements of an individual organization. The Enterprise Continuum is a view of the Architecture Repository that provides methods for classifying architecture and solution artifacts as they evolve from generic Foundation Architectures to Organization-Specific Architectures. The Enterprise Continuum comprises two complementary concepts: the Architecture Continuum and the Solutions Continuum.

The Enterprise Continuum and the Architecture Repository

The Enterprise Continuum provides a view of the Architecture Repository that shows the evolution of these related architectures from generic to specific, from abstract to concrete, and from logical to physical.

[Source: The TOGAF Standard, Version 9.2 Part V: Enterprise Continuum and Tools]

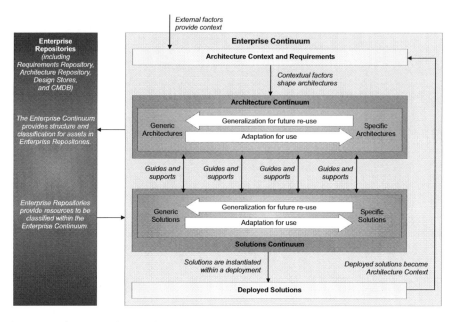

Figure 5:   The Enterprise Continuum

3.5 **The Architecture Repository**

(Syllabus Reference: Unit 2, Learning Outcome 4: You should be able to explain the core concept of the Architecture Repository.)

Supporting the Enterprise Continuum is the concept of an Architecture Repository, which can be used to store different classes of architectural output at different levels of abstraction, created by the ADM. In this way, the TOGAF standard facilitates understanding and co-operation between stakeholders and practitioners at different levels.

The structure of the TOGAF Architecture Repository is shown in Figure 6.

The major components within an Architecture Repository are as follows:

- The **Architecture Metamodel** describes the organizationally tailored application of an architecture framework, including a metamodel for architecture content
- The **Architecture Capability** defines the parameters, structures, and processes that support governance of the Architecture Repository
- The **Architecture Landscape** shows an architectural view of the building blocks that are in use within the organization today (e.g., a list of the

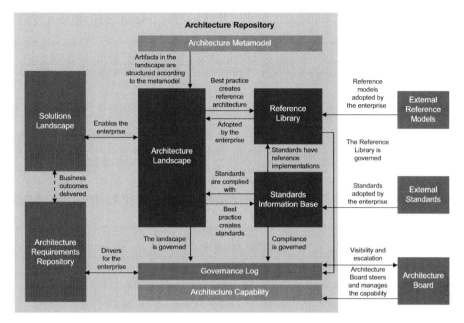

Figure 6:   TOGAF Architecture Repository Structure

live applications); the landscape is likely to exist at multiple levels of abstraction to suit different architecture objectives

- The **Standards Information Base (SIB)**[9] captures the standards with which new architectures must comply, which may include industry standards, selected products and services from suppliers, or shared services already deployed within the organization
- The **Reference Library** provides guidelines, templates, patterns, and other forms of reference material that can be leveraged in order to accelerate the creation of new architectures for the enterprise
- The **Governance Log** provides a record of governance activity across the enterprise
- The **Architecture Requirements Repository** provides a view of all authorized architecture requirements which have been agreed with the Architecture Board
- The **Solutions Landscape** presents an architectural representation of the SBBs supporting the Architecture Landscape which have been planned or deployed by the enterprise

---

9   An example SIB can be found on The Open Group website at www.opengroup.org/sib.

3.6 Establishing and Maintaining an Enterprise Architecture Capability

(Syllabus Reference: Unit 2, Learning Outcome 5: You should be able to explain the core concept of establishing and maintaining an Enterprise Architecture Capability.)

The Architecture Capability Framework is a set of reference materials and guidelines for establishing an architecture function or capability within an organization. A summary of the contents is shown in Table 7.

Table 7:   Architecture Capability Framework Contents Summary

Chapter	Description
Establishing an Architecture Capability	Guidelines for establishing an Architecture Capability within an organization.
Architecture Board	Guidelines for establishing and operating an enterprise Architecture Board.
Architecture Compliance	Guidelines for ensuring project compliance to architecture.
Architecture Contracts	Guidelines for defining and using Architecture Contracts.
Architecture Governance	Framework and guidelines for Architecture Governance.
Architecture Maturity Models	Techniques for evaluating and quantifying an organization's maturity in Enterprise Architecture.
Architecture Skills Framework	A set of role, skill, and experience norms for staff undertaking Enterprise Architecture work.

The structure for an Architecture Capability Framework is shown in Figure 7.

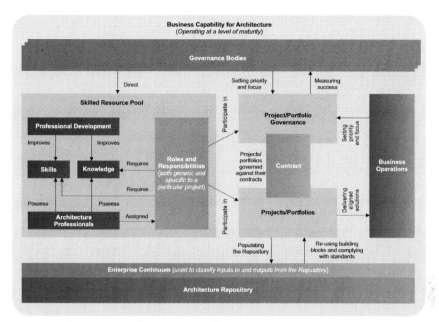

Figure 7:   Architecture Capability Framework

3.7 Establishing an Operational Architecture Capability

(Syllabus Reference: Unit 2, Learning Outcome 6: You should be able to explain the core concept of establishing the Architecture Capability as an operational entity.)

An Enterprise Architecture practice must be run like any other operational unit within a business; i.e., it should be treated like a business. To this end, and over and above the core processes defined within the ADM, an Enterprise Architecture practice should establish capabilities in the following areas:

- Financial Management
- Performance Management
- Service Management
- Risk Management
- Resource Management
- Communications and Stakeholder Management
- Quality Management
- Supplier Management
- Configuration Management
- Environment Management

Central to the notion of operating an ongoing architecture is the execution of well-defined and effective governance – Architecture Governance – whereby all architecturally significant activity is controlled and aligned within a single framework.

The benefits of Architecture Governance include:
- Increased transparency of accountability, and informed delegation of authority
- Controlled risk management
- Protection of the existing asset base through maximizing re-use of existing architectural components
- Proactive control, monitoring, and management mechanisms
- Process, concept, and component re-use across all organizational business units
- Value creation through monitoring, measuring, evaluation, and feedback
- Increased visibility supporting internal processes and external parties' requirements; in particular, increased visibility of decision-making at lower levels ensures oversight at an appropriate level within the enterprise of decisions that may have far-reaching strategic consequences for the organization
- Greater shareholder value; in particular, Enterprise Architecture increasingly represents the core intellectual property of the enterprise – studies have demonstrated a correlation between increased shareholder value and well-governed enterprises
- Integrates with existing processes and methodologies and complements functionality by adding control capabilities

3.8 Using the TOGAF Framework with Other Frameworks
(Syllabus Reference: Unit 2, Learning Outcome 7: You should be able to explain the core concept of the use of the TOGAF framework with other frameworks.)

Two of the key elements of any Enterprise Architecture framework are a definition of the deliverables that the architecting activity should produce, together with a description of the method for production.

Many Enterprise Architecture frameworks focus on the first of these – the specific set of deliverables – and are relatively silent about the methods to be used to generate them.

Because the TOGAF standard is a generic framework and intended to be used in a wide variety of environments, it provides a flexible and extensible content framework that underpins a set of generic architecture deliverables. As a result, the TOGAF framework may be used either in its own right, with the generic deliverables that it describes; or else these deliverables may be replaced or extended by a more specific set, defined in any other framework that the architect considers relevant.

In all cases, it is expected that the architect will adapt and build on the TOGAF framework in order to define a tailored method that is integrated into the processes and organization structures of the enterprise. This architecture tailoring may include adopting elements from other architecture frameworks, or integrating TOGAF methods with other standard frameworks, such as ITIL®, CMMI®, COBIT®, PRINCE2®, PMBOK®, and MSP®. It may also include adopting elements from reference materials in the TOGAF Library, such as the IT4IT™ Reference Architecture.

As a generic framework and method for Enterprise Architecture, the TOGAF standard also complements other frameworks that are aimed at specific vertical business domains, specific horizontal technology areas (such as security or manageability), or specific application areas (such as e-commerce).

> **Key Fact**
> Why is the TOGAF standard so popular in the industry?
> One key reason is that architects can use the TOGAF ADM in conjunction with any of the popular frameworks.
> The TOGAF ADM is framework-agnostic, and helps architects fill in the framework they might already have in use.
> [Source: Bill Estrem, "TOGAF to the Rescue" (www.opengroup.org/downloads)]

3.9 Summary

This chapter has introduced the core concepts of the TOGAF standard. This has included the following:

- The ADM and the purpose of each phase
- The concepts of deliverables, artifacts, and building blocks, and how they relate to the outputs of the ADM
- The Enterprise Continuum as a concept, and how it is used to classify artifacts
- The Architecture Repository and how it is used to store different classes of architectural output
- How to establish and maintain an Enterprise Architecture Capability, and the guidelines available within the TOGAF standard
- How to operate an Architecture Capability, including a list of recommended capabilities beyond the ADM
- The use of the TOGAF framework with other frameworks, and how the TOGAF framework may be used on its own or in conjunction with another framework

3.10 Test Yourself Questions

Q1:   Which of the TOGAF Architecture Development Method phases is the *initial* phase of an Architecture Development Cycle?

A.   Preliminary Phase
B.   Phase A
C.   Phase B
D.   Phase C
E.   Phase D

Q2:   Which of the TOGAF Architecture Development Method phases provides oversight of the implementation?

A.   Phase D
B.   Phase E
C.   Phase F
D.   Phase G
E.   Phase H

Q3.   Which of the TOGAF Architecture Development Method phases includes the creation and approval of the Architecture Vision document?
A.   Preliminary Phase
B.   Phase A
C.   Phase B
D.   Phase C
E.   Phase D

Q4.   Which of the following is *not* a phase of the ADM?
A.   Preliminary Phase
B.   Phase C: Requirements Architecture
C.   Phase F: Migration Planning
D.   Phase D: Technology Architecture
E.   Phase G: Implementation Governance

Q5:   Which of the following is defined as a work product that describes an aspect of an architecture?
A.   An artifact
B.   A building block
C.   A catalog
D.   A deliverable

Q6:   Complete the sentence: The Enterprise Continuum provides
_____
A.   An architecture framework
B.   A database of open industry standards
C.   Guidelines for developing a technical reference model
D.   Methods for classifying artifacts
E.   Techniques for developing architectures

Q7:   Which component of the Architecture Repository provides guidelines, templates, and patterns that can be used to create new architectures?
A.   The Architecture Metamodel
B.   The Architecture Capability
C.   The Architecture Landscape
D.   The Reference Library
E.   The Governance Log

3.11 Recommended Reading

The following are recommended sources of further information for this chapter:

- The TOGAF Standard, Version 9.2 Part I: Introduction, Core Concepts

Chapter 4

Key Terminology

4.1 Key Learning Points

This chapter will help you understand the key terminology of the TOGAF standard.

Key Points Explained

This chapter will help you to answer the following questions:
- What are the key terms for TOGAF 9 Foundation?
- Where are these terms used within this Study Guide?

The key terms listed and defined here are used in the rest of this Study Guide. The TOGAF 9 Foundation Syllabus expects candidates to be able to understand and explain the definitions marked as learning outcomes in this section, although notes that they are expected to be covered as part of the learning in other units. Please refer to this chapter when a term is used in other chapters and you need more information on its meaning.

4.2 Key Terms

(Syllabus Reference: Unit 3, Learning Outcomes 1-50: You should understand and be able to explain the following defined terms from the TOGAF standard.)

Application Architecture

(Syllabus Reference: Unit 3, Learning Outcome 1)

A description of the structure and interaction of the applications as groups of capabilities that provide key business functions and manage the data assets.

Architectural Style

(Syllabus Reference: Unit 3, Learning Outcome 2)

The combination of distinctive features related to the specific context within which architecture is performed or expressed; a collection of principles and characteristics that steer or constrain how an architecture is formed.

Architecture
(Syllabus Reference: Unit 3, Learning Outcome 3)
1. The fundamental concepts or properties of a system in its environment embodied in its elements, relationships, and in the principles of its design and evolution.
2. The structure of components, their inter-relationships, and the principles and guidelines governing their design and evolution over time

See also Chapter 2.

Architecture Building Block (ABB)
(Syllabus Reference: Unit 3, Learning Outcome 4)

A constituent of the architecture model that describes a single aspect of the overall model.

See also Building Block and Chapter 11.

Architecture Continuum
(Syllabus Reference: Unit 3, Learning Outcome 5)

A part of the Enterprise Continuum. A repository of architectural elements with increasing detail and specialization.

Note: This Continuum begins with foundational definitions such as reference models, core strategies, and basic building blocks. From there it spans to Industry Architectures and all the way to an organization's specific architecture.

See also Chapter 6.

Architecture Development Method (ADM)
(Syllabus Reference: Unit 3, Learning Outcome 6)

The core of the TOGAF framework. A multi-phase, iterative approach to develop and use an Enterprise Architecture to shape and govern business transformation and implementation projects.

See also Chapter 2, Chapter 5, and Chapter 7.

Architecture Domain
(Syllabus Reference: Unit 3, Learning Outcome 7)

The architectural area being considered. The TOGAF framework has four primary architecture domains within the TOGAF standard: Business, Data, Application, and Technology. Other domains may also be considered (e.g., Security).

> **BDAT (Business – Data – Application – Technology)**
> A simple mnemonic to aid remembering the four architecture domains.

Architecture Framework
(Syllabus Reference: Unit 3, Learning Outcome 8)

A conceptual structure used to plan, develop, implement, govern, and sustain an architecture.

See also Chapter 2.

Architecture Governance
(Syllabus Reference: Unit 3, Learning Outcome 9)

The practice of monitoring and directing architecture-related work. The goal is to deliver desired outcomes and adhere to relevant principles, standards, and roadmaps.

Architecture Principle
(Syllabus Reference: Unit 3, Learning Outcome 10)

A qualitative statement of intent that should be met by the architecture.

See also Chapter 8.

Architecture View
(Syllabus Reference: Unit 3, Learning Outcome 11)

A representation of a system from the perspective of a related set of concerns.

Note: View is sometimes used as a synonym for Architecture View.

Architecture Viewpoint
(Syllabus Reference: Unit 3, Learning Outcome 12)

A specification of the conventions for a particular kind of architecture view.

Note: Viewpoint is sometimes used as a synonym for Architecture Viewpoint.

Architecture Vision
(Syllabus Reference: Unit 3, Learning Outcome 13)

A succinct description of the Target Architecture that describes its business value and the changes to the enterprise that will result from its successful deployment. It serves as an aspirational vision and a boundary for detailed architecture development.

See also Chapter 7 and Chapter 12.

Artifact
(Syllabus Reference: Unit 3, Learning Outcome 14)

An architectural work product that describes an aspect of the architecture.

Baseline
(Syllabus Reference: Unit 3, Learning Outcome 15)

A specification that has been formally reviewed and agreed upon, that thereafter serves as the basis for further development or change and that can be changed only through formal change control procedures or a type of procedure such as configuration management.

Building Block
(Syllabus Reference: Unit 3, Learning Outcome 16)

A (potentially re-usable) component of enterprise capability that can be combined with other building blocks to deliver architectures and solutions.

Note: Building blocks can be defined at various levels of detail, depending on what stage of architecture development has been reached. For instance, at an early stage, a building block can simply consist of a name or an outline description. Later on, a building block may be decomposed into multiple supporting building blocks and may be accompanied by a full specification. Building blocks can relate to "architectures" or "solutions".

See also Section 3.3 and Chapter 11.

Business Architecture
(Syllabus Reference: Unit 3, Learning Outcome 17)

A representation of holistic, multi-dimensional business views of: capabilities, end-to-end value delivery, information, and organizational structure; and the relationships among these business views and strategies, products, policies, initiatives, and stakeholders.

See also Chapter 7.

Business Capability
(Syllabus Reference: Unit 3, Learning Outcome 18)

A particular ability that a business may possess or exchange to achieve a specific purpose.

Business Governance
(Syllabus Reference: Unit 3, Learning Outcome 19)

Concerned with ensuring that the business processes and policies (and their operation) deliver the business outcomes and adhere to relevant business regulation.

Capability
(Syllabus Reference: Unit 3, Learning Outcome 20)

An ability that an organization, person, or system possesses.

Concern
(Syllabus Reference: Unit 3, Learning Outcome 21)

An interest in a system relevant to one or more of its stakeholders.

See also Stakeholder and Chapter 10.

Course of Action
(Syllabus Reference: Unit 3, Learning Outcome 22)

Direction and focus provided by strategic goals and objectives, often to deliver the value proposition characterized in the business model.

Data Architecture
(Syllabus Reference: Unit 3, Learning Outcome 23)

A description of the structure and interaction of the enterprise's major types and sources of data, logical data assets, physical data assets, and data management resources.

See also Chapter 7.

Deliverable
(Syllabus Reference: Unit 3, Learning Outcome 24)

An architectural work product that is contractually specified and in turn formally reviewed, agreed, and signed off by the stakeholders.

Note: Deliverables represent the output of projects and those deliverables that are in documentation form will typically be archived at completion of a project, or transitioned into an Architecture Repository as a reference model, standard, or snapshot of the Architecture Landscape at a point in time.

See also Chapter 2 and Chapter 12.

Enterprise
(Syllabus Reference: Unit 3, Learning Outcome 25)

The highest level (typically) of description of an organization and typically covers all missions and functions. An enterprise will often span multiple organizations.

Enterprise Continuum

A categorization mechanism useful for classifying architecture and solution artifacts, both internal and external to the Architecture Repository, as they evolve from generic Foundation Architectures to Organization-Specific Architectures.

See also Chapter 6.

Foundation Architecture
(Syllabus Reference: Unit 3, Learning Outcome 26)

Generic building blocks, their inter-relationships with other building blocks, combined with the principles and guidelines that provide a foundation on which more specific architectures can be built.

See also Chapter 13.

Gap
(Syllabus Reference: Unit 3, Learning Outcome 27)

A statement of difference between two states. Used in the context of gap analysis, where the difference between the Baseline and Target Architecture is identified.

See also Chapter 8.

Governance
(Syllabus Reference: Unit 3, Learning Outcome 28)

The discipline of monitoring, managing, and steering a business (or IS/IT landscape) to deliver the business outcome required.

See also Chapter 9.

Information
(Syllabus Reference: Unit 3, Learning Outcome 29)

Any communication or representation of facts, data, or opinions, in any medium or form, including textual, numerical, graphic, cartographic, narrative, or audio-visual.

Information Technology (IT)
(Syllabus Reference: Unit 3, Learning Outcome 30)

1. The lifecycle management of information and related technology used by an organization.
2. An umbrella term that includes all or some of the subject areas relating to the computer industry, such as Business Continuity, Business IT Interface, Business Process Modeling and Management, Communication, Compliance and Legislation, Computers, Content Management, Hardware, Information Management, Internet, Offshoring, Networking, Programming and Software, Professional Issues, Project Management, Security, Standards, Storage, Voice and Data Communications. Various countries and industries employ other umbrella terms to describe this same collection.
3. A term commonly assigned to a department within an organization tasked with provisioning some or all of the domains described in (2) above.
4. Alternate names commonly adopted include Information Services, Information Management, etc.

Logical (Architecture)
(Syllabus Reference: Unit 3, Learning Outcome 31)

An implementation-independent definition of the architecture, often grouping related physical entities according to their purpose and structure; for example, the products from multiple infrastructure software vendors can all be logically grouped as Java® application server platforms.

Metadata
(Syllabus Reference: Unit 3, Learning Outcome 32)

Data about data, of any sort in any media, that describes the characteristics of an entity.

Metamodel
(Syllabus Reference: Unit 3, Learning Outcome 33)

A model that describes how and with what the architecture will be described in a structured way.

Method
(Syllabus Reference: Unit 3, Learning Outcome 34)

A defined, repeatable approach to address a particular type of problem.

Modeling
(Syllabus Reference: Unit 3, Learning Outcome 35)

A technique through construction of models which enables a subject to be represented in a form that enables reasoning, insight, and clarity concerning the essence of the subject matter.

Objective
(Syllabus Reference: Unit 3, Learning Outcome 36)

A time-bounded milestone for an organization used to demonstrate progress towards a goal; for example, "Increase Capacity Utilization by 30% by the end of 2019 to support the planned increase in market share".

Physical
(Syllabus Reference: Unit 3, Learning Outcome 37)

A description of a real-world entity. Physical elements in an Enterprise Architecture may still be considerably abstracted from Solution Architecture, design, or implementation views.

Reference Model (RM)
(Syllabus Reference: Unit 3, Learning Outcome 38)

A reference model is an abstract framework for understanding significant relationships among the entities of [an] environment, and for the development of consistent standards or specifications supporting that environment.

Note: A reference model is based on a small number of unifying concepts and may be used as a basis for education and explaining standards to a non-specialist. A reference model is not directly tied to any standards, technologies, or other concrete implementation details, but it does seek to provide common semantics that can be used unambiguously across and between different implementations.

See also Chapter 13.

Repository
(Syllabus Reference: Unit 3, Learning Outcome 39)

A system that manages all of the data of an enterprise, including data and process models and other enterprise information.

Requirement
(Syllabus Reference: Unit 3, Learning Outcome 40)

A statement of need that must be met by a particular architecture or work package.

Segment Architecture
A detailed, formal description of areas within an enterprise, used at the program or portfolio level to organize and align change activity.

Service

(Syllabus Reference: Unit 3, Learning Outcome 41)

1. A repeatable activity; a discrete behavior that a building block may be requested or otherwise triggered to perform.
2. An element of behavior that provides specific functionality in response to requests from actors or other services

Solution Architecture

(Syllabus Reference: Unit 3, Learning Outcome 42)

A description of a discrete and focused business operation or activity and how IS/IT supports that operation.

Note: A Solution Architecture typically applies to a single project or project release, assisting in the translation of requirements into a solution vision, high-level business and/or IT system specifications, and a portfolio of implementation tasks.

Solution Building Block

(Syllabus Reference: Unit 3, Learning Outcome 43)

A candidate solution which conforms to an Architecture Building Block (ABB).

See also Chapter 11.

Solutions Continuum

A part of the Enterprise Continuum. A repository of re-usable solutions for future implementation efforts. It contains implementations of the corresponding definitions in the Architecture Continuum.

See also Chapter 6.

Stakeholder

(Syllabus Reference: Unit 3, Learning Outcome 44)

An individual, team, organization, or class thereof, having an interest in a system.

See also Chapter 10.

Strategic Architecture
(Syllabus Reference: Unit 3, Learning Outcome 45)

A summary formal description of the enterprise, providing an organizing framework for operational and change activity, and an executive-level, long-term view for direction setting.

Target Architecture
(Syllabus Reference: Unit 3, Learning Outcome 46)

The description of a future state of the architecture being developed for an organization.

Note: There may be several future states developed as a roadmap to show the evolution of the architecture to a target state.

Technical Reference Model (TRM)
A structure which allows the components of an information system to be described in a consistent manner.

See also Chapter 13.

Technology Architecture
(Syllabus Reference: Unit 3, Learning Outcome 47)

A description of the structure and interaction of the technology services and technology components.

See also Chapter 7.

Transition Architecture
(Syllabus Reference: Unit 3, Learning Outcome 48)

A formal description of one state of the architecture at an architecturally significant point in time.

Note: One or more Transition Architectures may be used to describe the progression in time from the Baseline to the Target Architecture.

Value Stream
(Syllabus Reference: Unit 3, Learning Outcome 49)

A representation of an end-to-end collection of value-adding activities that create an overall result for a customer, stakeholder, or end user.

View
See Architecture View.

Viewpoint
See Architecture Viewpoint.

Viewpoint Library
(Syllabus Reference: Unit 3, Learning Outcome 50)

A collection of the specifications of architecture viewpoints contained in the Reference Library portion of the Architecture Repository.

4.3 Summary

This chapter lists and defines the key terms used in this Study Guide and the TOGAF 9 Foundation Syllabus. These terms are used as part of the learning outcomes within other chapters of this Study Guide.

4.4 Test Yourself Questions

Q1: Which one of the following is an architecture of generic services and functions?

    A. Application Architecture
    B. Foundation Architecture
    C. Segment Architecture
    D. Solution Architecture

Q2:   Which one of the following describes a statement of difference between two states?
      A.   Baseline
      B.   Constraint
      C.   Deliverable
      D.   Gap
      E.   Viewpoint

Q3:   Which one of the following is defined as a categorization mechanism for classifying architecture and solutions artifacts?
      A.   Architecture Principle
      B.   Architecture Repository
      C.   Enterprise Continuum
      D.   Foundation Architecture

Q4:   Which one of the following best defines an entity having an interest in a system?
      A.   Architect
      B.   Sponsor
      C.   Stakeholder

Q5:   Which one of the following is defined as formal description of the enterprise, providing an executive-level long-term view for direction setting?
      A.   Baseline Architecture
      B.   Business Architecture
      C.   Foundation Architecture
      D.   Segment Architecture
      E.   Strategic Architecture

Q6:   Which one of the following is defined as describing the state of an architecture at an architecturally significant point in time during the progression from the Baseline to the Target Architecture?
      A.   Capability Architecture
      B.   Foundation Architecture
      C.   Segment Architecture
      D.   Solution Architecture
      E.   Transition Architecture

4.5 Recommended Reading

The following are recommended sources of further information for this chapter:

- The TOGAF Standard, Version 9.2 Part I: Introduction, Definitions

Chapter 5

Introduction to the Architecture Development Method

5.1 Key Learning Points

This chapter describes the Architecture Development Method (ADM) cycle, what it consists of, its relationship to the rest of the TOGAF standard, and how to adapt and scope the ADM for use.

Key Points Explained

This chapter will help you to answer the following questions:

- What is the ADM cycle?
- What are the typical sets of steps within a phase?
- What is the versioning convention used for deliverables?
- What is its relationship to other parts of the TOGAF standard?
- What is the purpose of the supporting guidelines and techniques?
- What is the difference between guidelines and techniques?
- What are the key points of the ADM cycle?
- Why would I need to adapt the ADM to my enterprise?
- Why does the ADM process need to be governed?
- What are the major information areas covered by a governance repository?
- What are the reasons for scoping the architecture activity for my organization?
- What are the possible dimensions for limiting the scope?
- Why is there a need for an integration framework that sits above individual architectures?

5.2 The Architecture Development Cycle

(Syllabus Reference: Unit 4, Learning Outcome 1: You should be able to briefly describe the ADM cycle, its phases and the objective of each phase.)

The ADM consists of a number of phases that cycle through a range of architecture domains that enable the architect to ensure that a complex set of requirements is adequately addressed. The basic structure of the ADM is shown in Figure 8.

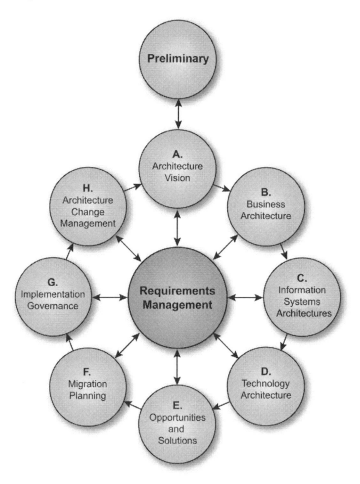

Figure 8:   The Architecture Development Method Cycle

The ADM is applied iteratively throughout the entire process, between phases, and within them. Throughout the ADM cycle, there should be frequent validation of results against the original requirements, both those for the whole ADM cycle, and those for the particular phase of the process. Such validation should reconsider scope, detail, schedules, and milestones. Each phase should consider assets produced from previous iterations of the process and external assets from the marketplace, such as other frameworks or models.

The ADM supports the concept of iteration at three levels:

- **Cycling around the ADM**: the ADM is presented in a circular manner indicating that the completion of one phase of architecture work directly feeds into subsequent phases of architecture work
- **Iterating between phases**: the TOGAF standard describes the concept of iterating across phases (e.g., returning to Business Architecture on completion of Technology Architecture)
- **Cycling around a single phase**: the ADM supports repeated execution of the activities within a single ADM phase as a technique for elaborating architectural content.

A summary of the activities by phase is shown in Table 8.

Table 8: Architecture Development Method Activities by Phase

ADM Phase	Activities
Preliminary Phase	Prepare the organization for successful TOGAF architecture projects. Undertake the preparation and initiation activities required to create an Architecture Capability, including the customization of the TOGAF framework, selection of tools, and the definition of Architecture Principles.
Requirements Management	Every stage of a TOGAF project is based on and validates business requirements. Requirements are identified, stored, and fed into and out of the relevant ADM phases, which dispose of, address, and prioritize requirements.
Phase A: Architecture Vision	Set the scope, constraints, and expectations for a TOGAF project. Create the Architecture Vision. Identify stakeholders. Validate the business context and create the Statement of Architecture Work. Obtain approvals.
Phase B: Business Architecture Phase C: Information Systems Architectures (Application & Data) Phase D: Technology Architecture	Develop architectures in four domains: 1. Business 2. Information Systems – Application 3. Information Systems – Data 4. Technology In each case, develop the Baseline and Target Architecture and analyze gaps.
Phase E: Opportunities & Solutions	Perform initial implementation planning and the identification of delivery vehicles for the building blocks identified in the previous phases. Determine whether an incremental approach is required, and if so identify Transition Architectures.

ADM Phase	Activities
Phase F: Migration Planning	Develop detailed Implementation and Migration Plan that addresses how to move from the Baseline to the Target Architecture.
Phase G: Implementation Governance	Provide architectural oversight for the implementation. Prepare and issue Architecture Contracts. Ensure that the implementation project conforms to the architecture.
Phase H: Architecture Change Management	Provide continual monitoring and a change management process to ensure that the architecture responds to the needs of the enterprise and maximizes the value of the architecture to the business.

Scoping an Enterprise Architecture Activity

The ADM defines a recommended sequence for the various phases and steps involved in developing an organization-wide Enterprise Architecture, but does not determine the scope for an Enterprise Architecture activity; this must be determined by the organization itself.

(Syllabus Reference: Unit 4, Learning Outcome 2: You should be able to describe a typical set of steps.)

The phases of the ADM cycle are further divided into steps; for example, the steps within the Business Architecture phase are as follows:

The steps shown are uniform for Phases B, C, and D. TOGAF 9 Foundation does not go into the detail of the contents of the steps within the ADM phases. That is a topic for the Level 2, TOGAF 9 Certified.

(Syllabus Reference: Unit 4, Learning Outcome 3: You should be able to describe the versioning convention for deliverables used in Phases A to D.)

Throughout the process of applying the ADM, outputs are generated. An output in an early phase may be modified in a later phase. The versioning of output is managed through version numbers.

In particular, a version numbering convention is used within the ADM to illustrate the evolution of Baseline and Target Architecture Definitions, as follows:

Phase	Deliverable	Content	Version	Description
A: Architecture Vision	Architecture Vision	Business Architecture	0.1	Version 0.1 indicates that a high-level outline of the architecture is in place.
		Data Architecture	0.1	
		Application Architecture	0.1	
		Technology Architecture	0.1	
B: Business Architecture	Architecture Definition Document	Business Architecture	1.0	Version 1.0 indicates a formally reviewed, detailed architecture.
C: Information Systems Architecture	Architecture Definition Document	Data Architecture	1.0	
		Application Architecture	1.0	
D: Technology Architecture	Architecture Definition Document	Technology Architecture	1.0	

ADM Output Versioning

The numbering scheme provided in the TOGAF ADM for its outputs is intended as an example. It should be adapted by the architect to meet the requirements of the organization and to work with the architecture tools and repositories employed by the organization.

5.3　What is the Relationship of the ADM to Other Parts of the TOGAF Standard?

(Syllabus Reference: Unit 4, Learning Outcome 4: You should be able to describe the relationship between the ADM and other parts of the TOGAF standard – the Enterprise Continuum, Architecture Repository, Foundation Architecture, and Supporting Guidelines and Techniques.)

This section explains the relationship between the ADM and other parts of the TOGAF standard.

5.3.1　Relationship to the Enterprise Continuum and Architecture Repository

The Enterprise Continuum is an approach for categorizing architectural source material – both the contents of the organization's own Architecture Repository, and the set of relevant, available reference models in the industry. The practical implementation of the Enterprise Continuum will typically take the form of an Architecture Repository that includes reference architectures, models, and patterns that have been accepted for use within the enterprise, and actual architectural work done previously within the enterprise.

At relevant places throughout the ADM, there are reminders to consider which architecture assets from the Architecture Repository the architect should use, if any. In some cases – for example, in the development of a Technology Architecture – this may be the TOGAF Foundation Architecture. Similarly, in the development of a Business Architecture, it may be a reference model for e-commerce taken from the industry at large.

While using the ADM, the architect is developing a snapshot of the enterprise's decisions and their implications at particular points in time. Each iteration of the ADM will populate an organization-specific landscape with all the architecture assets identified and leveraged through the process, including the final Organization-Specific Architecture delivered.

Architecture development is a continuous, cyclical process, and in executing the ADM repeatedly over time, the architect gradually adds more and more content to the organization's Architecture Repository. Although the primary focus of the ADM is on the development of the enterprise-specific architecture, in this wider context the ADM can also be viewed as the process of populating the enterprise's own Architecture Repository with relevant

re-usable building blocks taken from the "left", more generic side of the
Enterprise Continuum.

In fact, the first execution of the ADM will often be the hardest, since the
architecture assets available for re-use will be relatively scarce. Even at this
stage of development, however, there will be architecture assets available from
external sources such as the TOGAF standard, as well as the IT industry at
large, that could be leveraged in support of the effort.

Subsequent executions will be easier, as more and more architecture assets
become identified, are used to populate the organization's Architecture
Repository, and are thus available for future re-use.

5.3.2 The ADM and the Foundation Architecture

The ADM is also useful when populating the Foundation Architecture of an
enterprise. Business requirements of an enterprise may be used to identify
the necessary definitions and selections in the Foundation Architecture.
This could be a set of re-usable common models, policy and governance
definitions, or even as specific as overriding technology selections (e.g.,
if mandated by law). Population of the Foundation Architecture follows
similar principles as for an Enterprise Architecture, with the difference that
requirements for a whole enterprise are restricted to the overall concerns
and thus less complete than for a specific enterprise.

5.3.3 The ADM and Supporting Guidelines and Techniques

*(Syllabus Reference: Unit 4, Learning Outcome 5: You should be able to explain
the purpose of the supporting guidelines and techniques, and the difference
between guidelines and techniques.)*

The application of the ADM is supported by an extended set of resources
– guidelines, templates, checklists, and other detailed materials. These are
included in Part III: ADM Guidelines and Techniques, and in materials
referenced in the TOGAF Library.

The individual guidelines and techniques are described separately so that
they can be referenced from the relevant points in the ADM as necessary,
rather than having the detailed text clutter the description of the ADM itself.

Guidelines *versus* Technique

The guidelines provided to support the TOGAF standard describe how the ADM process can be adapted to deal with a number of different usage scenarios, including different process styles (e.g., the use of iteration) and also specific specialty architectures (such as security).

The techniques described support specific tasks within the ADM (e.g., the gap analysis technique, principles, business scenarios, etc.).

5.4 Key Points of the ADM Cycle

(Syllabus Reference: Unit 4, Learning Outcome 6: You should be able to briefly explain the key points of the ADM cycle.)

The TOGAF ADM is iterative. New decisions have to be taken at each iteration:

- Enterprise coverage
- Level of detail
- Time period
- Architecture asset re-use:
  — Previous ADM iterations
  — Other frameworks, system models, industry models, …

Decisions taken should be based on competence and/or resource availability, and the value accruing to the enterprise.

The ADM does not recommend the scope of activity; this has to be determined by the organization itself.

The choice of scope is critical to the success of the architecting effort. The main guideline is to focus on what creates value to the enterprise, and to select horizontal and vertical scope, and project schedules, accordingly. This exercise will be repeated, and future iterations will build on what is being created in the current effort, adding greater width and depth.

Where necessary, use of the ADM should be tailored to meet the needs of the organization. This means that some phases may be omitted, modified, or even additional procedures added.

5.5 How to Adapt the ADM to your Enterprise

(Syllabus Reference: Unit 4, Learning Outcome 7: You should be able to list the main reasons why you would need to adapt the ADM.)

The ADM is a generic method for architecture development, which is designed to deal with most system and organizational requirements. It easily copes with variable geographies, vertical sectors, and industry types. However, it will often be necessary to modify or extend the ADM to suit specific needs. One of the tasks before applying the ADM is to review the process and its outputs for applicability, and then tailor them as appropriate to the circumstances of the individual enterprise. This activity may well produce an "enterprise-specific" ADM.

There are a number of reasons for wanting to tailor the ADM to the circumstances of an individual enterprise. Some of the reasons are outlined as follows:

1. An important consideration is that the order of the phases in the ADM is to some extent dependent on the maturity of the architecture discipline within the enterprise concerned. For example, if the business case for doing architecture is not well recognized, then creating an Architecture Vision is essential; and a detailed Business Architecture needs to come next to define the business case for the remaining architecture work, and secure the active participation of key stakeholders in that work.

2. The order of phases may also be defined by the business and Architecture Principles of an enterprise. For example, the business principles may dictate that the enterprise be prepared to adjust its business processes to meet the needs of a packaged solution, so that it can be implemented quickly to enable fast response to market changes. In such a case, the Business Architecture (or at least the completion of it) may well follow completion of the Information Systems Architecture.

3. An enterprise may wish to use or tailor the ADM in conjunction with another Enterprise Architecture framework that has a defined set of deliverables specific to a particular vertical sector: Government, Defense, e-Business, Telecommunications, etc.

4. The ADM is one of many corporate processes that make up the corporate governance model for an enterprise. The ADM is complementary to, and supportive of, other standard program management processes. The

enterprise will tailor the ADM to reflect the relationships with, and dependencies on, the other management processes.

5. The ADM is being mandated for use by a prime or lead contractor in an outsourcing situation, and needs to be tailored to achieve a suitable compromise between the contractor's existing practices and the contracting enterprise's requirements.

6. The enterprise is a small-to-medium enterprise, and wishes to use a "cut-down" version of the ADM that is more attuned to the reduced level of resources and system complexity typical of such an environment.

7. The enterprise is very large and complex, comprising many separate but interlinked "enterprises" within an overall collaborative business framework, and the architecture method needs to be adapted to recognize this. Such enterprises usually cannot be treated successfully as a single entity and a more federated approach is required.

The ADM process can also be adapted to deal with a number of different use scenarios, including different process styles (e.g., the use of iteration) and also specific specialist architectures (such as security). These are discussed in Chapter 8.

5.6 The Need for Architecture Governance

(Syllabus Reference: Unit 4, Learning Outcome 8: You should be able to explain the need for the ADM process to be governed.)

The ADM, whether adapted by the organization or used as documented in the TOGAF standard, is a key process to be managed and governed. The Architecture Board should be satisfied that the method is being applied correctly across all phases of an architecture development iteration. Compliance with the ADM is fundamental to the governance of the architecture, to ensure that all considerations are made and all required deliverables are produced.

(Syllabus Reference: Unit 4, Learning Outcome 9: You should be able to describe the major information areas managed by a governance repository.)

The management of all architectural artifacts, governance, and related processes should be supported by a controlled environment. Typically this would be based on one or more repositories supporting versioned object and process control and status.

The major information areas managed by a governance repository should contain the following types of information:

- **Reference Data** (collateral from the organization's own repositories/ Enterprise Continuum, including external data; e.g., COBIT, the IT4IT Reference Architecture): used for guidance and instruction during project implementation
  This includes the details of information outlined above. The reference data includes a description of the governance procedures themselves.
- **Process Status**: a record of all information regarding the state of any governance processes; examples of this include outstanding compliance requests, dispensation requests, and compliance assessment investigations
- **Audit Information**: a record of all completed governance process actions
  This is used to support:
  - Key decisions and responsible personnel for any architecture project that has been sanctioned by the governance process
  - A reference for future architectural and supporting process developments, guidance, and precedence

5.7 Scoping the Architecture Activity for your Organization

(Syllabus Reference: Unit 4, Learning Outcome 10: You should be able to briefly explain the reasons for scoping an architecture activity.)

There are many reasons to constrain (or restrict) the scope of the architectural activity to be undertaken, most of which relate to limits in:

- The organizational authority of the team producing the architecture
- The objectives and stakeholder concerns to be addressed within the architecture
- The availability of people, finance, and other resources

The scope chosen for the architecture activity is normally directly dependent on available resources, and, in the final analysis, is usually a question of feasibility.

(Syllabus Reference: Unit 4, Learning Outcome 11: You should be able to list the possible dimensions for limiting the scope of an architecture activity.)

Table 9 shows the four dimensions in which the scope may be defined and limited.

Table 9:   Dimensions for Limiting the Scope of the Architecture Activity

Dimension	Considerations
Breadth	What is the full extent of the enterprise, and what part of that extent should the architecting effort deal with? Many enterprises are very large, effectively comprising a federation of organizational units that could validly be considered enterprises in their own right. The modern enterprise increasingly extends beyond its traditional boundaries, to embrace a fuzzy combination of traditional business enterprise combined with suppliers, customers, and partners.
Depth	To what level of detail should the architecting effort go? How much architecture is "enough"? What is the appropriate demarcation between the architecture effort and other, related activities (system design, system engineering, system development)?
Time period	What is the time period that needs to be articulated for the Architecture Vision, and does it make sense (in terms of practicality and resources) for the same period to be covered in the detailed architecture description? If not, how many Transition Architectures are to be defined, and what are their time periods?
Architecture domains	A complete Enterprise Architecture description should contain all four architecture domains (Business, Data, Application, Technology), but the realities of resource and time constraints often mean there is not enough time, funding, or resources to build a top-down, all-inclusive architecture description encompassing all four architecture domains, even if the enterprise scope is chosen to be less than the full extent of the overall enterprise.

Typically, the scope of an architecture is first expressed in terms of breadth, depth, and time. Once these dimensions are understood, a suitable combination of architecture domains can be selected that are appropriate to the problem being addressed.

5.8 Integrating the Architecture Domains for your Organization

(Syllabus Reference: Unit 4, Learning Outcome 12: You should be able to briefly explain the need for an integration framework that sits above individual architectures.)

Architectures that are created to address a subset of issues within an enterprise require a consistent frame of reference so that they can be considered as a group as well as point deliverables. The dimensions that are used to define the scope boundary of a single architecture (e.g., level of detail, architecture domain, etc.) are typically the same dimensions that must be addressed when considering the integration of many architectures. Figure 9 illustrates how different types of architecture need to co-exist.

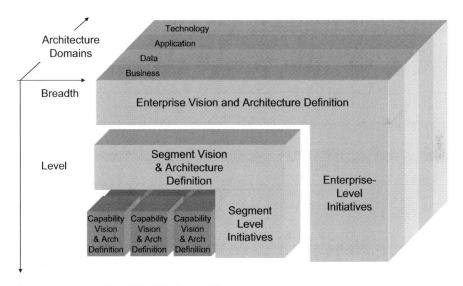

Figure 9:   Integration of Architecture Artifacts

At the present time, the state-of-the-art is such that architecture integration can only be accomplished at the lower end of the integration spectrum. Key factors to consider are the granularity and level of detail in each artifact, and the maturity of standards for the interchange of architectural descriptions.

5.9 Summary

The TOGAF ADM is a comprehensive general method that defines a recommended sequence for the various phases and steps involved in developing an architecture. It is an iterative method. A number of inputs and outputs are recommended for each phase. It draws on other parts of the TOGAF framework for assets and processes. The ADM can be used with other deliverables from other frameworks.

The ADM does not recommend a scope; this has to be determined by the organization itself. The choice of scope is critical to the success of the architecting effort. The main guideline is to focus on what creates value to the enterprise, and to select horizontal and vertical scope, and project schedules, accordingly. This exercise will be repeated, and future iterations will build on what is being created in the current effort, adding greater width and depth.

Where necessary, use of the ADM should be tailored to meet the needs of the organization. This means that some phases may be omitted, modified, or even additional procedures added.

5.10 Test Yourself Questions

Q1: Complete the sentence: Phase H _____

A. Prepares the organization for successful TOGAF architecture projects
B. Develops Baseline and Target Architectures and analyzes the gaps
C. Prepares and issues Architecture Contracts
D. Ensures that the architecture responds to the needs of the enterprise
E. All of these

Q2: Which of the following is the final step in development of the four architecture domains?

A. Conduct formal stakeholder review
B. Create Architecture Definition Document
C. Perform Gap Analysis
D. Select reference models, viewpoints, and tools

Q3:   Which of the following version numbers is used by the TOGAF
       standard as a convention to denote a high-level outline of an
       architecture?
       A.   Version 0
       B.   Version 0.1
       C.   Version 0.5
       D.   Version 1.0

Q4:   Which one of the following does *not* complete the sentence: When
       executing the ADM, the architect is not only developing a snapshot of
       the enterprise, but is also populating the _____
       A.   Architecture Repository
       B.   Architecture Capability Framework
       C.   Enterprise Continuum
       D.   Foundation Architecture

Q5:   Which of the following statements does *not* describe the phases of the
       ADM?
       A.   They are cyclical.
       B.   They are iterative.
       C.   Each phase refines the scope.
       D.   Each phase is mandatory.

Q6:   Which one of the following best describes a reason to adapt the ADM
       and take a federated approach?
       A.   The maturity of the architecture discipline within the enterprise
       B.   The use of the ADM in conjunction with another enterprise
             framework
       C.   The ADM is being used by a lead contractor in an outsourcing
             situation
       D.   The enterprise is very large and complex

Q7:   Which of the following are the major information areas managed by a
       governance repository?
       A.   Foundation Architectures, Industry Architectures, Organization-
             Specific Architectures
       B.   Standards Information Base, Architecture Landscape, Governance
             Log

    C.   Reference Data, Process Status, Audit Information

    D.   Application Architecture, Business Architecture, Data Architecture

Q8:   Which of these is *not* considered a dimension to consider when setting the scope of the architecture activity?

    A.   Architecture Domains

    B.   Breadth

    C.   Depth

    D.   Data Architecture

    E.   Time Period

5.11 Recommended Reading

The following are recommended sources of further information for this chapter:

- The TOGAF Standard, Version 9.2 Part II: ADM, Introduction to Part II

Chapter 6

The Enterprise Continuum and Tools

6.1 Key Learning Points

This chapter will help you understand the Enterprise Continuum, its purpose, and constituent parts. It also introduces the topic of tools standardization.

Key Points Explained

This chapter will help you to answer the following questions:
- What is the Enterprise Continuum?
- How is the Enterprise Continuum used in developing an architecture?
- How does the Enterprise Continuum promote re-use of architecture artifacts?
- What are the constituent pieces of the Enterprise Continuum?
- What is the Architecture Continuum?
- How is the Architecture Continuum used in developing an architecture?
- What is the relationship between the Architecture Continuum and the Solutions Continuum?
- What is the Solutions Continuum?
- How is the Solutions Continuum used to develop an architecture?
- What is the relationship between the Enterprise Continuum and the ADM?
- What is the Architecture Repository?
- What are the high-level issues with tools standardization?

Definition of "Continuum"

Noun: a continuous extent of something, no part of which is different from any other.

[Source: Wiktionary.org]

6.2 Overview of the Enterprise Continuum

(Syllabus Reference: Unit 5, Learning Outcome 1: You should be able to briefly explain what the Enterprise Continuum is.)

The Enterprise Continuum provides methods for classifying architecture and solution artifacts, both internal and external to the Architecture Repository, as they evolve from generic Foundation Architectures to Organization-Specific Architectures.

(Syllabus Reference: Unit 5, Learning Outcome 2: You should be able to explain how the Enterprise Continuum is used in organizing and developing an architecture.)

The Enterprise Continuum enables the architect to articulate the broad perspective of what, why, and how the Enterprise Architecture has been designed with the factors and drivers considered. The Enterprise Continuum is an important aid to communication and understanding, both within individual enterprises, and between customer enterprises and vendor organizations. Without an understanding of "where in the continuum you are", people discussing architecture can often talk at cross-purposes because they are referencing different points in the continuum at the same time, without realizing it.

The Benefits of a Consistent Language

Any architecture is context-specific; for example, there are architectures that are specific to individual customers, industries, subsystems, products, and services. Architects, on both the buy-side and supply-side, must have at their disposal a consistent language to effectively communicate the differences between architectures. Such a language enables engineering efficiency and the effective use of Commercial Off-The-Shelf (COTS) product functionality. The Enterprise Continuum provides that consistent language.

6.3 The Enterprise Continuum and Architecture Re-Use

(Syllabus Reference: Unit 5, Learning Outcome 3: You should be able to explain how the Enterprise Continuum promotes re-use of architecture artifacts.)

The Enterprise Continuum enables the organization of re-usable architecture artifacts and solution assets to maximize the Enterprise Architecture investment opportunities.

The "virtual repository" that is the Enterprise Continuum consists of all the architecture assets; that is, models, patterns, architecture descriptions, and other artifacts produced during application of the ADM. These can exist both within the enterprise and in the IT industry at large, and are considered the set of assets available for the development of architectures for the enterprise.

The deliverables of previous architecture work, which are available for re-use, are examples of internal architecture and solutions artifacts. Examples of external architecture and solution artifacts include the wide variety of industry reference models and architecture patterns that exist, and are continually emerging, including those that are highly generic (such as the TOGAF Technical Reference Model (TRM)); those specific to certain aspects of IT (such as a web services architecture, or a generic manageability architecture); those specific to certain types of information processing (such as e-commerce); and those specific to certain vertical industries, such as the models generated by vertical consortia like the TM Forum (in the Telecommunications sector), ARTS (Retail), Energistics® (Petrotechnical), etc.

The Enterprise Architecture determines which architecture and solution artifacts an organization includes in its Architecture Repository. Re-use is a major consideration in this decision.

6.4 The Constituent Parts of the Enterprise Continuum
(Syllabus Reference: Unit 5, Learning Outcome 4: You should be able to describe the constituent parts of the Enterprise Continuum.)

The Enterprise Continuum consists of three parts as described below, and illustrated in Figure 5. Each of the three parts is considered to be a distinct continuum.

6.4.1 The Enterprise Continuum
(Syllabus Reference: Unit 5, Learning Outcome 5: You should be able to explain the purpose of the Enterprise Continuum.)

The Enterprise Continuum is the outermost continuum and classifies assets related to the context of the overall Enterprise Architecture.

The Enterprise Continuum classes of assets may influence architectures, but are not directly used during the ADM architecture development. The Enterprise Continuum classifies contextual assets used to develop architectures, such as policies, standards, strategic initiatives, organizational structures, and enterprise-level capabilities. The Enterprise Continuum can also classify solutions (as opposed to descriptions or specifications of solutions). Finally, the Enterprise Continuum contains two specializations, namely the Architecture and Solutions Continuum.

6.4.2 The Architecture Continuum

The Architecture Continuum offers a consistent way to define and understand the generic rules, representations, and relationships in an architecture, including traceability and derivation relationships (e.g., to show that an Organization-Specific Architecture is based on an industry or generic standard).

The Architecture Continuum represents a structuring of Architecture Building Blocks (ABBs) which are re-usable architecture assets. ABBs evolve through their development lifecycle from abstract and generic entities to fully expressed Organization-Specific Architecture assets. The Architecture Continuum assets will be used to guide and select the elements in the Solutions Continuum (see below).

The Architecture Continuum shows the relationships among foundational frameworks (such as the TOGAF framework), Common Systems Architectures (such as the III-RM), Industry Architectures, and Enterprise Architectures. The Architecture Continuum is a useful tool to discover commonality and eliminate unnecessary redundancy.

6.4.3 The Solutions Continuum

The Solutions Continuum provides a consistent way to describe and understand the implementation of the assets defined in the Architecture Continuum. The Solutions Continuum defines what is available in the organizational environment as re-usable Solution Building Blocks (SBBs). The solutions are the results of agreements between customers and business partners that implement the rules and relationships defined in the architecture space. The Solutions Continuum addresses the commonalities and differences among the products, systems, and services of implemented systems.

6.5 The Architecture Continuum in Detail

(Syllabus Reference: Unit 5, Learning Outcome 6: You should be able to explain the purpose of the Architecture Continuum.)

There is a continuum of architectures, Architecture Building Blocks (ABBs), and architecture models that are relevant to the task of constructing an enterprise-specific architecture, that are termed by the TOGAF standard as the Architecture Continuum. These are shown in Figure 10.

Figure 10:   The Architecture Continuum

(Syllabus Reference: Unit 5, Learning Outcome 7: You should be able to list the stages of architecture evolution defined in the Architecture Continuum.)

Figure 10 illustrates how architectures are developed and evolved across a continuum ranging from Foundation Architectures, such as the TOGAF® Series Guide: The TOGAF Technical Reference Model (TRM), through Common Systems Architectures, and Industry Architectures, and to an enterprise's own Organization-Specific Architectures.

The arrows in the Architecture Continuum represent the relationship that exists between the different architectures in the Architecture Continuum. The leftwards direction focuses on meeting enterprise needs and business requirements, while the rightwards direction focuses on leveraging architectural components and building blocks.

The enterprise needs and business requirements are addressed in increasing detail from left to right. The architect will typically look to find re-usable architecture elements toward the left of the continuum. When elements are not found, the requirements for the missing elements are passed to the left of the continuum for incorporation.

Within the Architecture Continuum there are a number of re-usable Architecture Building Blocks (ABBs) – the models of architectures.

6.5.1 Foundation Architecture

A Foundation Architecture consists of generic components, inter-relationships, principles, and guidelines that provide a foundation on which more specific architectures can be built.

6.5.2 Common Systems Architectures

Common Systems Architectures guide the selection and integration of specific services from the Foundation Architecture to create an architecture useful for building common solutions across a wide number of relevant domains. Examples of Common Systems Architectures include Security Architecture, Management Architecture, Network Architecture, etc.

The TOGAF® Series Guide: The TOGAF Integrated Information Infrastructure Reference Model (III-RM) is a reference model that supports describing Common Systems Architecture in the Application domain that focuses on the requirements, building blocks, and standards relating to the vision of Boundaryless Information Flow.

6.5.3 Industry Architectures

Industry Architectures guide the integration of common systems components with industry-specific components, and guide the creation of industry solutions for specific customer problems within a particular industry.

A typical example of an industry-specific component is a data model representing the business functions and processes specific to a particular vertical industry, such as the Retail industry's "Active Store" architecture, or an Industry Architecture that incorporates the Energistics data model (www.energistics.org).

6.5.4 Organization-Specific Architectures

Organization-Specific Architectures describe and guide the final deployment of user-written or third-party components that constitute effective solutions for particular enterprises.

6.6 The Solutions Continuum in Detail

(Syllabus Reference: Unit 5, Learning Outcome 8: You should be able to explain the purpose of the Solutions Continuum.)

The Solutions Continuum, shown in Figure 11, represents the implementations of the architectures at the corresponding levels of the Architecture Continuum. At each level in the Solutions Continuum there is a set of reference building blocks that represent a solution to the business requirements at that level. A populated Solutions Continuum can be regarded as a re-use library.

Figure 11:   The Solutions Continuum

In Figure 11, moving from left-to-right is focused on providing solution value; that is, foundation solutions provide value in creating common systems solutions. Common systems solutions value is used to create industry solutions, and industry solutions are used to create organization-specific solutions. The right-to-left direction increasingly focuses on addressing enterprise needs.

(Syllabus Reference: Unit 5, Learning Outcome 9: You should be able to list the stages of architecture evolution defined in the Solutions Continuum.)

The solution types within the Solutions Continuum are looked at in detail in the following sections.

6.6.1 Foundation Solutions

Foundation Solutions are highly generic concepts, tools, products, services, and solution components that are the fundamental providers of capabilities. Services include professional services – such as training and consulting services – that ensure the maximum investment value from solutions in the shortest possible time; and support services – such as Help Desk – that ensure the maximum possible value from solutions (services that ensure timely updates and upgrades to the products and systems).

Example Foundation Solutions would include programming languages, operating systems, foundational data structures (such as EDIFACT), generic approaches to organization structuring, foundational structures for organizing IT operations (such as ITIL or the IT4IT Reference Architecture), etc.

6.6.2 Common Systems Solutions

A Common Systems Solution is an implementation of a Common Systems Architecture and is comprised of a set of products and services. It represents the highest common denominator for one or more solutions in the industry segments that the Common Systems Solution supports.

Common Systems Solutions represent collections of common requirements and capabilities, rather than those specific to a particular customer or industry. Common Systems Solutions provide organizations with operating environments specific to operational and informational needs, such as high availability transaction processing and scalable data warehousing systems. Examples of Common Systems Solutions include: an enterprise management system product and a security system product.

Computer systems vendors are the typical providers of technology-centric Common Systems Solutions. "Software as a service" vendors are typical providers of common application solutions. Business process outsourcing vendors are typical providers of business capability-centric Common Systems Solutions.

6.6.3 Industry Solutions

An Industry Solution is an implementation of an Industry Architecture, which provides re-usable packages of common components and services specific to an industry.

Fundamental components are provided by Common Systems Solutions and/or Foundation Solutions, and are augmented with industry-specific components. Examples include a physical database schema or an industry-specific point-of-service device.

Industry Solutions are industry-specific, aggregate procurements that are ready to be tailored to an individual organization's requirements.

In some cases an industry solution may include not only an implementation of the Industry Architecture, but also other solution elements, such as specific products, services, and systems solutions that are appropriate to that industry.

6.6.4 Organization-Specific Solutions

An Organization-Specific Solution is an implementation of the Organization-Specific Architecture that provides the required business functions. Because solutions are designed for specific business operations, they contain the highest amount of unique content in order to accommodate the varying people and processes of specific organizations.

Building Organization-Specific Solutions on Industry Solutions, Common Systems Solutions, and Foundation Solutions is the usual way of connecting the Architecture Continuum to the Solutions Continuum, as guided by the architects within an enterprise.

An Organization-Specific Solution will be structured in order to support specific Service-Level Agreements (SLAs) to ensure support of the operational systems at desired service levels. For example, a third-party application hosting provider may offer different levels of support for operational systems. These agreements would define the terms and conditions of that support.

Other key factors to be defined within an Organization-Specific Solution are the key operating parameters and quality metrics that can be used to monitor and manage the environment.

6.6.5 The Relationship of the Architecture Continuum to the Solutions Continuum

The relationship between the Architecture Continuum and the Solutions Continuum is one of guidance, direction, and support. For example, Foundation Architectures guide the creation or selection of Foundation Solutions. Foundation Solutions support the Foundation Architecture by helping to realize the architecture defined in the Architecture Continuum. The Foundation Architecture also guides development of Foundation Solutions, by providing architectural direction, requirements and principles that guide selection, and realization of appropriate solutions. A similar relationship exists between the other elements of the Enterprise Continuum.

The relationships depicted in Figure 12 are a best case for the ideal use of architecture and solution components.

Figure 12:   The Enterprise Continuum

6.7 Using the Enterprise Continuum within the ADM

(Syllabus Reference: Unit 5, Learning Outcome 10: You should be able to explain the relationship between the Enterprise Continuum and the TOGAF ADM.)

The TOGAF ADM describes the process of developing an enterprise-specific architecture and an enterprise-specific solution which conform to that architecture by adopting and adapting (where appropriate) generic architectures and solutions. In a similar fashion, specific architectures and solutions that prove to be credible and effective will be generalized for re-use. At relevant places throughout the TOGAF ADM, there are pointers to useful architecture assets at the relevant level of generality in the continuum classification. These assets include reference models from The Open Group and industries at large. The TOGAF Library provides reference models for consideration for use in developing an Organization-Specific Architecture.

6.8 The Architecture Repository

(Syllabus Reference: Unit 5, Learning Outcome 11: You should be able to describe the Architecture Repository.)

Operating a mature Architecture Capability within a large enterprise creates a huge volume of architectural output. Effective management and leverage of these architectural work products require a formal taxonomy for different types of architectural asset alongside dedicated processes and tools for architectural content storage.

The TOGAF standard provides a structural framework for an Architecture Repository that allows an enterprise to distinguish between different types of architectural assets that exist at different levels of abstraction in the organization. This Architecture Repository is one part of the wider Enterprise Repository, which provides the capability to link architectural assets to components of the Detailed Design, Deployment, and Service Management Repositories.

(Syllabus Reference: Unit 5, Learning Outcome 12: You should be able to explain the relationship between the Enterprise Continuum and the Architecture Repository.)

The Architecture Repository is a model for a physical instance of the Enterprise Continuum.

Figure 13:   TOGAF Architecture Repository Structure

(Syllabus Reference: Unit 5, Learning Outcome 13: You should be able to describe the classes of information held in the Architecture Repository.)

At a high level, the following classes of architectural information are expected to be held within an Architecture Repository:

- The **Architecture Metamodel** describes the organizationally tailored application of an architecture framework, including a method for architecture development and a metamodel for architecture content
- The **Architecture Capability** defines the parameters, structures, and processes that support governance of the Architecture Repository
- The **Architecture Landscape** presents an architectural representation of assets in use, or planned, by the enterprise at particular points in time
- The **Standards Information Base** captures the standards with which new architectures must comply, which may include industry standards, selected products and services from suppliers, or shared services already deployed within the organization

- The **Reference Library** provides guidelines, templates, patterns, and other forms of reference material that can be leveraged in order to accelerate the creation of new architectures for the enterprise
- The **Governance Log** provides a record of governance activity across the enterprise
- The **Architecture Requirements Repository** provides a view of all authorized architecture requirements which have been agreed with the Architecture Board
- The **Solutions Landscape** presents an architectural representation of the SBBs supporting the Architecture Landscape which have been planned or deployed by the enterprise

6.8.1 The Architecture Landscape

(Syllabus Reference: Unit 5, Learning Outcome 14: You should be able to list the three levels of the Architecture Landscape.)

The Architecture Landscape holds architectural views of the state of the enterprise at particular points in time. Due to the sheer volume and the diverse stakeholder needs throughout an entire enterprise, the Architecture Landscape is divided into three levels of granularity:

1. Strategic Architectures show a long-term summary view of the entire enterprise. Strategic Architectures provide an organizing framework for operational and change activity and allow for direction setting at an executive level.
2. Segment Architectures provide more detailed operating models for areas within an enterprise. Segment Architectures can be used at the program or portfolio level to organize and operationally align more detailed change activity.
3. Capability Architectures show in a more detailed fashion how the enterprise can support a particular unit of capability. Capability Architectures are used to provide an overview of current capability, target capability, and capability increments and allow for individual work packages and projects to be grouped within managed portfolios and programs.

6.8.2 The Standards Information Base

(Syllabus Reference: Unit 5, Learning Outcome 15: You should be able to explain the purpose of the Standards Information Base within the Architecture Repository.)

The Standards Information Base is a repository area that holds a record of the set of specifications, to which architectures must conform.

Establishment of a Standards Information Base provides an unambiguous basis for architectural governance since:

- The standards are easily accessible to projects and therefore the obligations of the project can be understood and planned for
- Standards are stated in a clear and unambiguous manner, so that compliance can be objectively assessed

6.9 Tools Standardization

To manage the content of the Enterprise Continuum we need tools in order to:

- Promote re-use
- Enable sharing of architecture information within an organization
- Facilitate easier maintenance of the architecture
- Ensure common terminology is used
- Provide stakeholders with relevant models

Using the models within the TOGAF standard, it is then possible to implement the Architecture Repository in a tool, thereby responding to stakeholder enquiries for models, views, and other queries.

6.10 Summary

The Enterprise Continuum provides methods for classifying architecture and solution artifacts, both internal and external to the Architecture Repository, as they evolve from generic Foundation Architectures to Organization-Specific Architectures. It is also an aid to communication between all architects involved in building and procuring an architecture by providing a common language and terminology. This, in turn, enables efficiency in engineering and effective use of COTS products.

The Architecture Continuum is part of an organization's Enterprise Continuum and is supported by the Solutions Continuum. It offers a consistent way to define and understand the generic rules, representations, and relationships in an information system, and it represents a conceptual structuring of re-usable architecture assets.

The Architecture Continuum shows the relationships among Foundation Architectures (such as the TOGAF TRM), Common Systems Architectures (such as the III-RM), Industry Architectures, and Organization-Specific Architectures. It is also a useful method to discover commonality and eliminate unnecessary redundancy.

The Solutions Continuum is part of an organization's Enterprise Continuum. It represents implementations of the architectures at the corresponding levels of the Architecture Continuum. At each level, the Solutions Continuum is a population of the architecture with reference building blocks – either purchased products or built components – that represent a solution to the enterprise's business needs.

The Architecture Repository provides a structural framework for a physical repository for managing architectural work products and is a model of a physical instance of the Enterprise Continuum. The Architecture Repository defines classes for architectural information held in the repository.

The TOGAF standard recognizes the need to manage the content of the Enterprise Continuum using tools, and includes high-level guidance on standardization of tools.

6.11 Test Yourself Questions

Q1:   Which of the following statements does *not* apply to the Enterprise Continuum?

    A.   It is a repository of all known architecture assets and artifacts in the IT industry.

    B.   It is a view of the Architecture Repository.

    C.   It provides methods for classifying architecture and solution assets.

      D.   It is an important aid to communication for architects on both the buy and supply-side.

      E.   It is an aid to organization of re-usable and solution assets.

Q2:   Which of the following in the Enterprise Continuum is an example of an internal architecture or solution artifact that is available for re-use?

      A.   Deliverables from previous architecture work

      B.   Industry reference models and patterns

      C.   The TOGAF TRM

      D.   The ARTS data model

Q3:   Which of the following best completes the next sentence: The Enterprise Continuum aids communication _____

      A.   Within enterprises

      B.   With vendor organizations

      C.   By providing a consistent language to communicate the differences between architectures

      D.   All of these

Q4:   Which of the following are considered to be the constituent parts of the Enterprise Continuum?

      A.   Standards Information Base, Governance Log

      B.   TOGAF TRM, III-RM

      C.   Architecture Continuum, Solutions Continuum

      D.   Business Architecture, Application Architecture

Q5:   Complete the sentence: The TOGAF Integrated Information Infrastructure Reference Model (III-RM) can be classified in the Architecture Continuum as a(n) _____

      A.   Common Systems Architecture

      B.   Industry Architecture

      C.   Enterprise Architecture

      D.   Foundation Architecture

Q6:   Which of the following responses does *not* complete the next sentence? The Solutions Continuum _____

      A.   Provides a way to understand the implementation of assets defined in the Architecture Continuum

B.   Addresses the commonalities and differences among the products, systems, and services of an implemented system

C.   Can be considered to have at each level a set of building blocks that represent a solution to the business requirements at that level

D.   Contains a number of re-usable Architecture Building Blocks

E.   Has a relationship to the Architecture Continuum that includes guidance, direction, and support

Q7:   Which one of the following reference building blocks is *not* part of the Solutions Continuum?

A.   Systems libraries

B.   Organization-specific solutions

C.   Foundation solutions

D.   Common systems solutions

E.   Industry solutions

Q8:   Which of the following is considered a model for a physical instance of the Enterprise Continuum?

A.   The Architecture Repository

B.   The III-RM

C.   The Standards Information Base

D.   The TOGAF TRM

Q9:   Which class of architectural information held within the Architecture Repository would contain adopted reference models?

A.   Architecture Metamodel

B.   Architecture Capability

C.   Standards Information Base

D.   Reference Library

Q10: Which level of the Architecture Landscape contains the most detail?

A.   Capability Architectures

B.   Segment Architectures

C.   Strategic Architectures

Q11: Which of the following describes a purpose of a Standards Information Base?

    A.   To provide a method for architecture development

    B.   To provide a basis for architectural governance

    C.   To provide a record of governance activity

    D.   To show an architectural view of building blocks

6.12 Recommended Reading

The following are recommended sources of further information for this chapter:

- The TOGAF Standard, Version 9.2 Part V: Enterprise Continuum and Tools

Chapter 7

The ADM Phases

7.1 Key Learning Points

This chapter will help you understand how each of the ADM phases contributes to the success of Enterprise Architecture.

Key Points Explained

This chapter will help you to answer the following questions:

- What are the objectives of each of the ADM phases?
- What are the key aspects to the approach taken in each phase for Enterprise Architecture development?

7.2 Preliminary Phase

The Preliminary Phase includes the preparation and initiation activities to create an Architecture Capability. Key activities are as follows:

- Understand the business environment
- Ensure high-level management commitment
- Obtain agreement on scope
- Establish Architecture Principles
- Establish governance structure
- Customization of the TOGAF framework

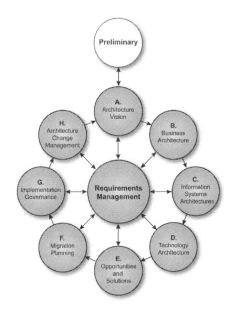

7.2.1 Objectives

(Syllabus Reference: Unit 6, Learning Outcome P.1: You should be able to describe the main objectives of the Preliminary Phase.)

- Determine the Architecture Capability desired by the organization:
  — Review the organizational context for conducting Enterprise Architecture
  — Identify and scope the elements of the enterprise organizations affected by the Architecture Capability
  — Identify the established frameworks, methods, and processes that intersect with the Architecture Capability
  — Establish a Capability Maturity target
- Establish the Architecture Capability:
  — Define and establish the Organizational Model for Enterprise Architecture
  — Define and establish the detailed process and resources for Architecture Governance
  — Select and implement tools that support the Architecture Capability
  — Define the Architecture Principles (see Chapter 8 for more information on Architecture Principles)

7.2.2 Approach
(Syllabus Reference: Unit 6, Learning Outcome P.2: You should be able to briefly explain the seven aspects of the approach undertaken in the Preliminary Phase.)

The Preliminary Phase is about defining "where, what, why, who, and how we do architecture" in the enterprise concerned. The main aspects are as follows:
- Defining the enterprise
- Identifying key drivers and elements in the organizational context
- Defining the requirements for architecture work
- Defining the Architecture Principles that will inform any architecture work
- Defining the framework to be used
- Defining the relationships between management frameworks
- Evaluating the Enterprise Architecture's maturity

Defining the Enterprise
One of the main challenges of Enterprise Architecture is that of enterprise scope. The scope of the enterprise, and whether it is federated, will determine those stakeholders who will derive most benefit from the new or enhanced Enterprise Architecture. It is imperative to appoint a sponsor at this stage to ensure that the resultant activity has resources to proceed and the clear support of the business management. The enterprise may include many

organizations and the duties of the sponsor are to ensure that all stakeholders are included in defining, establishing, and using the Architecture Capability.

Identifying Key Drivers and Elements in the Organizational Context

It is necessary to understand the context surrounding the architecture. For example, considerations include:

- The commercial models and budget for the Enterprise Architecture
- The stakeholders
- The intentions and culture of the organization
- Current processes that support execution of change and operation of the enterprise
- The Baseline Architecture landscape
- The skills and capabilities of the enterprise

Review of the organizational context should provide valuable requirements on how to tailor the architecture framework, particularly the level of formality, the expenditure required, and contact with other organizations.

Defining the Requirements for Architecture Work

Business imperatives drive the requirements and performance metrics. One or more of the following requirements need to be articulated so that the sponsor can identify the key decision-makers and stakeholders involved in defining and establishing the Architecture Capability:

- Business requirements
- Cultural aspirations
- Organization intents
- Strategic intent
- Forecast financial requirements

Defining the Architecture Principles that will Inform any Architecture Work

The definition of Architecture Principles is fundamental to the development of an Enterprise Architecture. Architecture work is informed by business principles as well as Architecture Principles. The Architecture Principles themselves are also normally based in part on business principles.

Architecture Principles are covered in further detail in Chapter 8.

Defining the Framework to be Used

The ADM is a generic method, intended to be used by enterprises in a wide variety of industry types and geographies. It can also be used with a wide variety of other Enterprise Architecture frameworks, if required. The TOGAF framework has to co-exist with and enhance the operational capabilities of other frameworks in use within an organization. The main frameworks that may need to be coordinated with the TOGAF framework are:

- **Business Capability Management** (Business Direction and Planning) which determine what business capabilities are required
- **Portfolio/Project Management Methods** which determine how a company manages its change initiatives
- **Operations Management Methods** which describe how a company runs its day-to-day operations, including IT
- **Solution Development Methods** which formalize the way that business systems are delivered

As illustrated in Figure 14, these frameworks are not discrete, and there are significant overlaps between them and the Business Capability Management. Consequently, an Enterprise Architect must be aware of the impact that the architecture has on the entire enterprise.

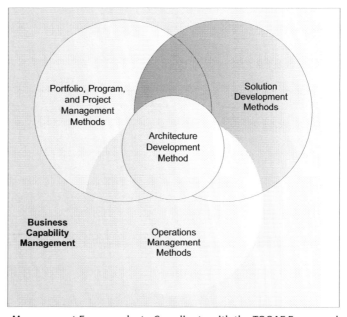

Figure 14:   Management Frameworks to Coordinate with the TOGAF Framework

Defining the Relationships between Management Frameworks

Figure 15 shows a more detailed set of dependencies between the various frameworks and business planning activity. The Enterprise Architecture can be used to provide a structure for all of the corporate initiatives.

Figure 15:   Interoperability and Relationships between Management Frameworks

The management frameworks are required to complement each other and work in close harmony for the good of the enterprise.

Evaluating the Enterprise Architecture Maturity

Capability Maturity Models (CMMs) are a good way of assessing the ability of an enterprise to exercise different capabilities. Capability Maturity Models typically identify selected factors that are required to exercise a capability. An organization's ability to execute specific factors provides a measure of maturity and can be used to recommend a series of sequential steps to improve a capability. It is an assessment that gives executives an insight into pragmatically improving a capability.

7.3 Phase A: Architecture Vision

Phase A is about project establishment and initiates an iteration of the Architecture Development Cycle, setting the scope, constraints, and . expectations for the iteration.

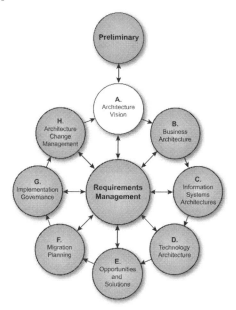

It is required at the start of every architecture cycle in order to create the Architecture Vision, validate the business context, and create the approved Statement of Architecture Work.

7.3.1 Objectives

(Syllabus Reference: Unit 6, Learning Outcome A.1: You should be able to describe the main objectives of Phase A.)

- Develop a high-level aspirational vision of the capabilities and business value to be delivered as a result of the proposed Enterprise Architecture
- Obtain approval for a Statement of Architecture Work that defines a program of works to develop and deploy the architecture outlined in the Architecture Vision

7.3.2 Approach

(Syllabus Reference: Unit 6, Learning Outcome A.2: You should be able to briefly explain the two main aspects of the approach for Phase A.)

Phase A starts with receipt of a Request for Architecture Work from the sponsoring organization to the architecture organization. A key objective is to ensure proper recognition and endorsement from corporate management, and the support and commitment of line management for this evolution of the ADM cycle.

As the name of the phase suggests, creating the Architecture Vision is a key activity in this phase. This is discussed below, as is the business scenarios technique which can be used to develop the Architecture Vision.

Creating the Architecture Vision

The Architecture Vision provides the sponsor with a key tool to sell the benefits of the proposed capability to stakeholders and decision-makers within the enterprise. It describes how the new capability will meet the business goals and strategic objectives and address the stakeholder concerns when implemented. Integral to the Architecture Vision is an understanding of emerging technologies and their potential impact on industries and enterprises, without which many business opportunities may be missed.

Normally, key elements of the Architecture Vision – such as the enterprise mission, vision, strategy, and goals – have been documented as part of some wider business strategy or enterprise planning activity that has its own lifecycle within the enterprise. In such cases, the activity in Phase A is concerned with verifying and understanding the documented business strategy and goals. Phase A may also integrate the enterprise strategy and goals with the strategy and goals implicit within the current architecture. Business models are key strategy artifacts that can provide such a perspective, by showing how the organization intends to deliver value to its customers and stakeholders.

In other cases, little or no Business Architecture work may have been done to date. In such cases, there will be a need for the architecture team to research, verify, and gain buy-in to the key business objectives and processes that the architecture is to support. This may be done as a free-standing exercise, either preceding architecture development, or as part of the ADM initiation phase (Preliminary Phase). This exercise should examine and search for existing materials related to fundamental Business Architecture concepts, such as business capabilities, value streams, and organization maps.

In addition, the Architecture Vision should explore other domains appropriate for the Enterprise Architecture; e.g., information, security, digital, etc.

Business scenarios (see below) are an appropriate and useful technique to discover and document business requirements, and to articulate an Architecture Vision that responds to those requirements.

The Architecture Vision provides a first-cut, high-level description of the Baseline and Target Architectures, covering the Business, Data, Application, and Technology domains. These outline descriptions are developed in subsequent phases.

Once an Architecture Vision is defined and documented in the Statement of Architecture Work, it is critical to use it to build a consensus. Without this consensus it is very unlikely that the final architecture will be accepted by the organization as a whole. The consensus is represented by the sponsoring organization signing the Statement of Architecture Work.

Business Scenarios

The business scenarios technique can be used for identifying and articulating the business requirements implied, and the implied architecture requirements. This technique is described in detail in Chapter 8. The technique may be used iteratively, at different levels of detail in the hierarchical decomposition of the Business Architecture.

7.4 Phase B: Business Architecture

Phase B is about development of a Business Architecture to support an agreed Architecture Vision. This describes the fundamental organization of a business embodied in:

- Its business process and people
- Their relationships to each other and the people
- The principles governing its design and evolution and shows how an organization meets its business goals

7.4.1 Objectives

(Syllabus Reference: Unit 6,
Learning Outcome B.1: You should be able to describe the main objectives of Phase B.)

- Develop the Target Business Architecture that describes how the enterprise needs to operate to achieve the business goals, and respond to the strategic drivers set out in the Architecture Vision, in a way that addresses the Statement of Architecture Work and stakeholder concerns
- Identify candidate Architecture Roadmap components based upon gaps between the Baseline and Target Business Architectures

7.4.2 Approach

(Syllabus Reference: Unit 6, Learning Outcome B.2: You should be able to explain the main aspects of the approach in Phase B.)

Business Architecture is a representation of holistic, multi-dimensional business views of: capabilities, end-to-end value delivery, information, and organizational structure; and the relationships among these business views and strategies, products, policies, initiatives, and stakeholders. In summary, the Business Architecture relates business elements to business goals and elements of other domains.

General

A knowledge of the Business Architecture is a prerequisite for architecture work in any other domain (Data, Application, Technology), and is therefore the first architecture activity that needs to be undertaken.

In practical terms, the Business Architecture is often necessary as a means of demonstrating the business value of subsequent architecture work to key stakeholders, and the return on investment to those stakeholders from supporting and participating in the subsequent work.

The Architecture Vision (developed in Phase A) primarily determines the scope of the work in Phase B. The business strategy defines the goals and drivers and metrics for success, but not necessarily how to get there. That is the role of the Business Architecture, defined in detail in Phase B.

Developing the Baseline Description

If an enterprise has existing architecture descriptions, they should be used as the basis for the Baseline Description. Some input may have been used already in Phase A in developing the Architecture Vision, and may be sufficient for this baseline. Where no such descriptions exist, information will have to be gathered and architecture descriptions developed.

Techniques for developing appropriate architecture descriptions are as follows:

Applying Business Capabilities

The business capability map found or developed in Phase A provides a self-contained view of the business that is independent of the current organizational structure, business processes, information systems and applications, and the rest of the product or service portfolio. Those business capabilities should be mapped back to the organizational units, value streams, information systems, and strategic plans within the scope of the Enterprise Architecture project.

Applying Value Streams

Value streams provide valuable stakeholder context into why the organization needs business capabilities, while business capabilities provide what the organization needs for a particular value stage to be successful. A value stream can be analyzed within the scope of the project through heat mapping (by value stream stage) or by developing use-cases around a complete definition of the value stream (see Baseline Example in the TOGAF® Series Guide: Value Streams). A project might focus on specific stakeholders, one element of business value, or stress some stages over others to develop better requirements for solutions in later phases. A recommended technique is mapping relationships between the stages in a value stream to business capabilities, and then performing a gap analysis for capabilities in the context of the business value achieved by the value stream for a specific stakeholder.

Applying the Organization Map

The Organization Map is a key element of Business Architecture because it provides the organizational context for the whole Enterprise Architecture effort. While capability mapping exposes what a business does and value stream mapping exposes how it delivers value to specific stakeholders, the Organization Map identities the business units or third parties that possess or use those capabilities and which participate in the value streams. Together with capability maps and value streams, the Organization Map provides an understanding of which business units to involve in the architecture effort, who and when to talk about a given requirement, and how to measure the impact of various decisions.

Applying Business Modeling

In addition to the techniques described above (capability maps, value streams, and organization maps), a variety of other modeling techniques may be used. For example, **Activity Models** (also called **Business Process Models**), **Use-Case Models**, and **Class Models.** All three types of model can be represented in the Unified Modeling Language (UML), and a variety of tools exist for generating such models. The Defense sector also uses **Node Connectivity Diagrams** and **Information Exchange Matrices**.

Using the Architecture Repository

The architecture team will need to consider what relevant Business Architecture resources are available from the Architecture Repository, in particular:

- Industry reference models (in terms of the Enterprise Continuum) relevant to the organization's industry sector
- Enterprise-specific Business Architecture views (capability maps, value stream maps, organization maps, etc.)
- Enterprise-specific building blocks (process components, business rules, job descriptions, etc.)
- Applicable standards

7.5 Phase C: Information Systems Architectures

Phase C is about documenting the Information Systems Architectures for an architecture project, including the development of Data and Application Architectures. This describes the major types of information and the application systems that process the infor- mation, and their relationships to each other and the environment.

It involves some combination of Data and Application Architecture, which may be developed either sequentially or concurrently:

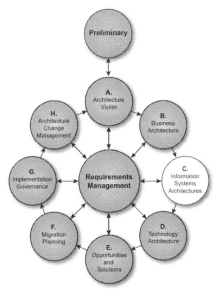

- Data Architecture
- Application Architecture

7.5.1 Objectives

(Syllabus Reference: Unit 6, Learning Outcome C.1: You should be able to describe the main objectives of Phase C.)

- Develop the Target Information Systems (Data and Application) Architecture, describing how the enterprise's Information Systems Architecture will enable the Business Architecture and the Architecture Vision, in a way that addresses the Statement of Architecture Work and stakeholder concerns
- Identify candidate Architecture Roadmap components based upon gaps between the Baseline and Target Information Systems (Data and Application) Architectures

Consistency of Phases B, C, and D

As noted in Section 5.2, the architectures developed in Phases B, C, and D follow a uniform step pattern, including development of Baseline and Target Architecture descriptions and analysis of the gaps. The details are out of scope for TOGAF 9 Foundation, and are covered instead in Level 2.

7.5.2 Approach

(Syllabus Reference: Unit 6, Learning Outcome C.2: You should be able to briefly explain the approach recommended by the TOGAF standard for Phase C.)

Phase C involves some combination of Data and Application Architecture, in either order. Advocates exist for both sequences, and the TOGAF standard leaves this to the user to decide. Consideration of the factors is outside the scope of the TOGAF 9 Foundation Syllabus. The syllabus covers the two topics below.

Key Considerations for the Data Architecture

Key considerations for the Data Architecture include:

- Data Management

  When an enterprise has chosen to undertake large-scale architectural transformation, it is important to understand and address data management issues. A structured and comprehensive approach to data management enables the effective use of data to capitalize on its competitive advantages.

  Considerations include:

  — Defining application components which will serve as the system of record or reference for enterprise master data

  — Defining enterprise-wide standards that all application components, including software packages, need to adopt

  — Understanding how data entities are utilized by business functions, processes, and services

  — Understanding how and where enterprise data entities are created, stored, transported, and reported

  — Understanding the level and complexity of data transformations required to support the information exchange needs between applications

  — Defining the requirement for software in supporting data integration with the enterprise's customers and suppliers (e.g., use of ETL[10] tools during the data migration, data profiling tools to evaluate data quality, etc.)

- Data Migration

  When an existing application is replaced, there will be a critical need to migrate data (master, transactional, and reference) to the new application. The Data Architecture should identify data migration requirements and also provide indicators as to the level of transformation, weeding, and cleansing that will be required to present data in a format that meets the requirements and constraints of the target application. The objective is to ensure that the target application has quality data when it is populated. Another key consideration is to ensure that an enterprise-wide common data definition is established to support the transformation.

---

10   ETL is an abbreviation for Extract, Transform, and Load.

- Data Governance
  Considerations for data governance should ensure that the enterprise
  has the necessary dimensions in place to enable the transformation, as
  follows:
  — **Structure**: Does the enterprise have the necessary organizational
    structure and the standards bodies to manage data entity aspects of
    the transformation?
  — **Management System**: Does the enterprise have the necessary
    management system and data-related programs to manage the
    governance aspects of data entities throughout its lifecycle?
  — **People**: What data-related skills and roles does the enterprise require
    for the transformation? If the enterprise lacks such resources and
    skills, the enterprise should consider either acquiring those critical
    skills or training existing internal resources to meet the requirements
    through a well-defined learning program.

Using the Architecture Repository

As part of this phase, the architecture team should consider what relevant
Data Architecture and Application Architecture resources are available in the
organization's Architecture Repository; in particular, generic models relevant
to the organization's industry "vertical" sector. For example:

- Data Architecture models:
  — ARTS has defined a data model for the Retail industry
  — Energistics has defined a data model for the Petrotechnical industry
- Application Architecture models:
  — The TM Forum – www.tmforum.org – has developed detailed
    applications models relevant to the Telecommunications industry
  — The Open Group has developed a detailed application architecture
    reference model for the IT segment of organizations (the IT4IT
    Reference Architecture)
  — The Object Management Group (OMG) – www.omg.org – has
    a number of vertical Domain Task Forces developing software
    models relevant to specific vertical domains such as Healthcare,
    Transportation, Finance, etc.
  — Application models relevant to common high-level business
    functions, such as electronic commerce, supply chain management,
    etc.

The Open Group has a Reference Model for Integrated Information Infrastructure (III-RM) – see the TOGAF® Series Guide: The TOGAF Integrated Information Infrastructure Reference Model (III-RM) – that focuses on the application-level components and services necessary to provide an integrated information infrastructure.

7.6 Phase D: Technology Architecture

Phase D is about documenting the Technology Architecture for an architecture project, in the form of the fundamental organization of the IT systems:

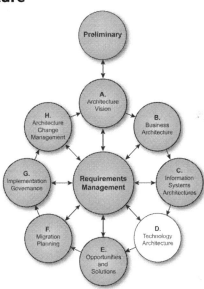

- Embodied in the hardware, software, and communications technology
- Their relationships to each other and the environment
- The principles governing its design and evolution

7.6.1 Objectives

(Syllabus Reference: Unit 6, Learning Outcome D.1: You should be able to describe the main objectives of Phase D.)

- Develop the Target Technology Architecture that enables the Architecture Vision, target business, data, and application building blocks to be delivered through technology components and technology services, in a way that addresses the Statement of Architecture Work and stakeholder concerns
- Identify candidate Architecture Roadmap components based upon gaps between the Baseline and Target Technology Architectures

7.6.2 Approach

(Syllabus Reference: Unit 6, Learning Outcome D.2: You should be able to briefly explain the approach to Phase D.)

Emerging Technologies – A Driver for Change
The evolution of new technologies is a major driver for change in enterprises looking for new innovative ways of operating and improving their business. The Technology Architecture needs to capture the transformation opportunities available to the enterprise through the adoption of new technology.

While the Enterprise Architecture is led by the business concerns, drivers for change are often found within evolving technology capabilities. As more digital innovations reach the market, stakeholders need to both anticipate and be open to technology-driven change. Part of Digital Transformation has arisen due to the convergence of telecommunications and computer capabilities, which have opened up new ways of implementing infrastructures.

The flexibility of the TOGAF ADM enables technology change to become a driver and strategic resource rather than a recipient of Change Requests. As a result, the Technology Architecture may both drive business capabilities and respond to information system requirements at the same time.

Using the Architecture Repository
As part of Phase D, the architecture team must consider what relevant Technology Architecture resources are available in the Architecture Repository. In particular, consider:

- Existing IT services
- The adopted technical reference model, if applicable
- Generic technology models relevant to the organization's industry "vertical" sector; for example, in the Telecommunications industry such models have been developed by the TM Forum
- Technology models relevant to Common Systems Architectures; for example, the III-RM

7.7 Phase E: Opportunities and Solutions

Phase E is the first phase which is directly concerned with implementation. It describes the process of identifying major implementation projects and grouping them into work packages that deliver the Target Architecture identified in previous phases.

Key activities are as follows:

- Perform initial implementation planning
- Identify the major implementation projects
- Group changes into work packages
- Decide on approach:
  — Make *versus* buy *versus* re-use
  — Outsource
  — COTS
  — Open Source
- Assess priorities
- Identify dependencies

7.7.1 Objectives

(Syllabus Reference: Unit 6, Learning Outcome E.1: You should be able to describe the main objectives of Phase E.)

- Generate the initial complete version of the Architecture Roadmap, based upon the gap analysis and candidate Architecture Roadmap components from Phases B, C, and D
- Determine whether an incremental approach is required, and if so identify Transition Architectures that will deliver continuous business value
- Define the overall Solution Building Blocks (SBBs) to finalize the Target Architecture based on the Architecture Building Blocks (ABBs)

7.7.2 Approach
(Syllabus Reference: Unit 6, Learning Outcome E.2: You should be able to briefly explain the approach to Phase E.)

Phase E concentrates on how to deliver the architecture. It takes into account the complete set of gaps between the Target and Baseline Architectures in all architecture domains, and logically groups changes into work packages within the enterprise's portfolios. This is an effort to build a best-fit roadmap that is based upon the stakeholder requirements, the enterprise's business transformation readiness, identified opportunities and solutions, and identified implementation constraints. The key is to focus on the final target while realizing incremental business value.

Phase E is the initial step on the creation of a well considered Implementation and Migration Plan that is integrated into the enterprise's portfolio in Phase F.

There are four key concepts in the transition from developing to delivering a Target Architecture:
- Architecture Roadmap
- Work Packages
- Transition Architectures
- Implementation and Migration Plan

The Architecture Roadmap lists individual work packages in a timeline that will realize the Target Architecture. Each work package identifies a logical group of changes necessary to realize the Target Architecture. A Transition Architecture describes the enterprise at an architecturally significant state between the Baseline and Target Architectures. Transition Architectures provide interim Target Architectures upon which the organization can converge. The Implementation and Migration Plan provides a schedule of the projects that will realize the Target Architecture.

7.8 Phase F: Migration Planning

Phase F addresses detailed migration planning; that is, how to move from the Baseline to the Target Architectures.

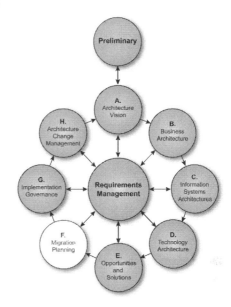

Key activities include:

- For work packages and projects identified, perform a cost/benefit analysis and a risk assessment
- Finalize a detailed Implementation and Migration Plan

7.8.1 Objectives

(Syllabus Reference: Unit 6, Learning Outcome F.1: You should be able to describe the main objectives for Phase F.)

- Finalize the Architecture Roadmap and the supporting Implementation and Migration Plan
- Ensure that the Implementation and Migration Plan is coordinated with the enterprise's approach to managing and implementing change in the enterprise's overall change portfolio
- Ensure that the business value and cost of work packages and Transition Architectures is understood by key stakeholders

7.8.2 Approach

(Syllabus Reference: Unit 6, Learning Outcome F.2: You should be able to briefly explain the approach to Phase F.)

The focus of Phase F is the creation of an Implementation and Migration Plan in co-operation with the portfolio and project managers. Phase E provides an incomplete Architecture Roadmap and Implementation and Migration Plan that address the Statement of Architecture Work. In Phase F this Roadmap and the Implementation and Migration Plan are integrated with the enterprise's other change activity. Activities include assessing the dependencies, costs, and benefits of the various migration projects. The Architecture Roadmap, and Implementation and Migration Plan, from Phase E will form the basis of the detailed Implementation and Migration Plan that will include portfolio and project-level detail. The Architecture Development Cycle should then be completed, and lessons learned documented to enable continuous process improvement.

7.9 Phase G: Implementation Governance

Phase G defines how the architecture constrains the implementation projects, monitors it while building it, and produces a signed Architecture Contract.

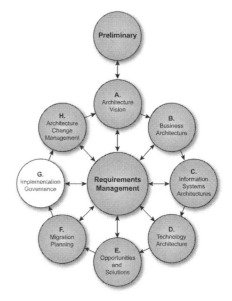

Key activities include:
- Provide architectural oversight for the implementation
- Define architecture constraints on implementation projects
- Govern and manage an Architecture Contract
- Monitor implementation work for conformance

7.9.1 Objectives
(Syllabus Reference: Unit 6, Learning Outcome G.1: You should be able to describe the main objectives of Phase G.)
- Ensure conformance with the Target Architecture by implementation projects
- Perform appropriate Architecture Governance functions for the solution and any implementation-driven architecture Change Requests

7.9.2 Approach
(Syllabus Reference: Unit 6, Learning Outcome G.2: You should be able to briefly explain the approach to Phase G.)

In Phase G all the information for successful management of the various implementation projects is brought together. The actual development occurs in parallel with Phase G.

The approach in Phase G is to:

- Establish an implementation program that will enable the delivery of the agreed Transition Architectures
- Adopt a phased deployment schedule that reflects the business priorities embodied in the Architecture Roadmap
- Follow the organization's standard for corporate, IT, and Architecture Governance
- Use the organization's established portfolio/program management approach, where this exists
- Define an operations framework to ensure the effective long life of the deployed solution

A key aspect of Phase G is ensuring compliance with the defined architecture(s), not only by the implementation projects, but also by other ongoing projects.

7.10 Phase H: Architecture Change Management

Phase H ensures that changes to the architecture are managed in a controlled manner.

Key activities include:

- Provide continual monitoring and a change management process
- Ensure that changes to the architecture are managed in a cohesive and architected way
- Provide flexibility to evolve rapidly in response to changes in the technology or business environment
- Monitor the business and capacity management

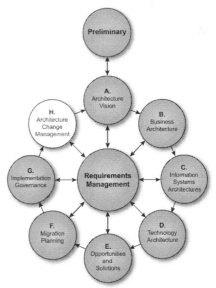

7.10.1 Objectives

(Syllabus Reference: Unit 6, Learning Outcome H.1: You should be able to describe the main objectives of Phase G.)

- Ensure that the architecture lifecycle is maintained
- Ensure that the Architecture Governance Framework is executed
- Ensure that the enterprise's Architecture Capability meets current requirements

7.10.2 Approach

(Syllabus Reference: Unit 6, Learning Outcome H.2: You should be able to briefly explain the approach to Phase H.)

The goal of an architecture change management process is to ensure that the architecture achieves its original target business value. Monitoring business growth and decline is a critical aspect of this phase.

The value and change management process, once established, will determine:

- The circumstances under which the Enterprise Architecture, or parts of it, will be permitted to change after deployment, and the process by which that will happen
- The circumstances under which the Architecture Development Cycle will be initiated to develop a new architecture

Drivers for Change

There are three ways to change the existing infrastructure that have to be integrated:

1. Strategic, top-down directed change to enhance or create new capability (capital)
2. Bottom-up changes to correct or enhance capability (operations and maintenance) for infrastructure under operations management
3. Experiences with the previously delivered project increments in the care of operations management, but still being delivered by ongoing projects

Enterprise Architecture Change Management Process

The Enterprise Architecture change management process needs to determine how changes are to be managed, what techniques are to be applied, and what methodologies used.

The TOGAF standard recommends the following approach based on classifying the required architectural changes into one of three categories:

- **Simplification change**: a simplification change can normally be handled via change management techniques
- **Incremental change**: an incremental change may be capable of being handled via change management techniques, or it may require partial re-architecting, depending on the nature of the change (see Guidelines for Maintenance *versus* Architecture Redesign for guidance)
- **Re-architecting change**: a re-architecting change requires putting the whole architecture through the Architecture Development Cycle again

Another way of looking at these three choices is as follows:

- A simplification change to an architecture is often driven by a requirement to reduce investment
- An incremental change is driven by a requirement to derive additional value from existing investment
- A re-architecting change is driven by a requirement to increase investment in order to create new value for exploitation

To determine whether a change is simplification, incremental, or re-architecting, the following activities are undertaken:

- Registration of all events that may impact the architecture
- Resource allocation and management for architecture tasks
- The process or role responsible for architecture resources has to make an assessment of what should be done
- Evaluation of impacts

Guidelines for Maintenance *versus* Architecture Redesign

Suggested guidelines are:

- If the change impacts two stakeholders or more, then it is likely to require an architecture redesign and re-entry to the ADM
- If the change impacts only one stakeholder, then it is more likely to be a candidate for change management
- If the change can be allowed under a dispensation, then it is more likely to be a candidate for change management

For example:
- If the impact is significant for the business strategy, then there may be a need to re-do the whole Enterprise Architecture – thus a re-architecting approach
- If a new technology or a standard emerges, then there may be a need to refresh the Technology Architecture, but not the whole Enterprise Architecture – thus an incremental change
- If the change is at an infrastructure level – for example, ten systems reduced or changed to one system – this may not change the architecture above the physical layer, but it will change the Baseline Description of the Technology Architecture; this would be a simplification change handled via change management techniques

In particular, a refreshment cycle (partial or complete re-architecting) may be required if:
- The Foundation Architecture needs to be re-aligned with the business strategy
- Substantial change is required to components and guidelines for use in deployment of the architecture
- Significant standards used in the product architecture are changed which have significant end-user impact; e.g., regulatory changes

If there is a need for a refreshment cycle, then a new Request for Architecture Work must be issued (to move to another cycle).

7.11 Requirements Management

(Syllabus Reference: Unit 6, Learning Outcome R.1: You should be able to briefly explain how Requirements Management fits into the ADM cycle.)

The process of managing architecture requirements applies to all phases of the ADM cycle. The Requirements Management process is a dynamic process, which addresses the identification of requirements for the enterprise, stores them, and then feeds them in and out of the relevant ADM phases.

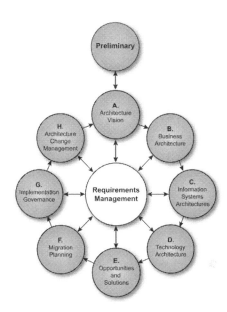

As shown by its central placement in the ADM cycle diagram, this process is central to driving the ADM process.

7.11.1 Objectives

(Syllabus Reference: Unit 6, Learning Outcome R.2: You should be able to describe the nature of the Requirements Management process.)

- Ensure that the Requirements Management process is sustained and operates for all relevant ADM phases
- Manage architecture requirements identified during any execution of the ADM cycle or a phase
- Ensure that the relevant architecture requirements are available for use by each phase as the phase is executed

7.11.2 Approach

(Syllabus Reference: Unit 6, Learning Outcome R.3: You should be able to describe the approach to Requirements Management.)

The ADM is continuously driven by the Requirements Management process. The ability to deal with changes in requirements is crucial, as architecture by its nature deals with uncertainty and change, bridging the divide between the aspirations of the stakeholders and what can be delivered as a practical solution.

> **Requirements Management Manages the Flow of Requirements**
> Note that the Requirements Management process itself does not dispose of, address, or prioritize any requirements; this is done within the relevant phase of the ADM.

It is recommended that an Architecture Requirements Repository is used to record and manage all architecture requirements. The TOGAF standard does not mandate or recommend any specific process or tool for requirements management; it simply states what an effective Requirements Management process should achieve, which could be thought of as "the requirements for requirements".

The TOGAF standard suggests a number of resources in this area:

Business Scenarios
Business scenarios are an appropriate and useful technique to discover and document business requirements, and to describe an Architecture Vision that responds to those requirements. Business scenarios are described in detail in the TOGAF® Series Guide: Business Scenarios.

Other Requirements Tools
There is a large and increasing number of Commercial Off-The-Shelf (COTS) tools available for the support of requirements management. The Volere website has a useful list of requirements tools (see www.volere.co.uk/tools.htm).

7.12 Summary

This chapter has described each of the ADM phases and how they contribute to the development of an Enterprise Architecture. This has included the key objectives for each phase, together with high-level considerations for the approach.

7.13 Test Yourself Questions

Q1: Which of the ADM phases includes the development of Application
and Data Architectures?
A. Phase A
B. Phase B
C. Phase C
D. Phase D
E. Phase E

Q2: Which of the ADM phases includes the objective of establishing the
organizational model for Enterprise Architecture?
A. Preliminary
B. Phase A
C. Phase B
D. Phase D
E. Phase E

Q3: Which one of the following is an objective of Phase A?
A. To review the stakeholders, their requirements, and priorities
B. To develop a high-level vision of the business value to be delivered
C. To generate and gain consensus on an outline Implementation and
Migration Strategy
D. To formulate recommendations for each implementation project

Q4: Complete the sentence: According to the TOGAF standard, all of the
following are part of the approach to the Preliminary Phase, *except*

_____

A. Creating the Architecture Vision
B. Defining the enterprise
C. Defining the framework to be used
D. Evaluating the Enterprise Architecture maturity

Q5: Which one of the following is a recommended way to evaluate the
Enterprise Architecture maturity?
A. Architecture Principles
B. Business Scenarios
C. Capability Maturity Models
D. Risk Management

Q6:   Which of the ADM phases commences with receipt of a Request for
      Architecture Work from the sponsor?
      A.   Preliminary
      B.   Phase A
      C.   Phase E
      D.   Phase G
      E.   Phase H

Q7:   Which of the following is a technique that can be used to discover and
      document business requirements in Phase A?
      A.   Business Scenarios
      B.   Business Transformation Readiness Assessment
      C.   Gap Analysis
      D.   Stakeholder Management

Q8:   Which architecture domain is the first architecture activity undertaken
      in the ADM cycle?
      A.   Application
      B.   Business
      C.   Data
      D.   Technology

Q9:   Which one of the following is considered a relevant resource for Phase
      B available from the Architecture Repository?
      A.   The ARTS data model
      B.   Business rules, job descriptions
      C.   The III-RM
      D.   The TOGAF Technical Reference Model

Q10: Which one of the following is a potential resource in Phase C and
      is a reference model focusing on application-level components and
      services?
      A.   The ARTS data model
      B.   Business rules, job descriptions
      C.   The III-RM
      D.   The TOGAF Technical Reference Model

Q11: In which ADM phase is an outline Implementation and Migration Strategy generated?
    A.   Phase E
    B.   Phase F
    C.   Phase G
    D.   Phase H

Q12: In which ADM phase are the Transition Architectures defined in Phase E confirmed with the stakeholders?
    A.   Phase E
    B.   Phase F
    C.   Phase G
    D.   Phase H

Q13: In which ADM phase is an Architecture Contract developed to cover the overall implementation and deployment process?
    A.   Phase E
    B.   Phase F
    C.   Phase G
    D.   Phase H

Q14: Which one of the following is an objective of Phase H: Architecture Change Management?
    A.   Finalize the Architecture Roadmap
    B.   Manage architecture requirements identified during execution of the ADM cycle
    C.   Perform Architecture Governance functions for the solution
    D.   Operate the Architecture Governance Framework

Q15: Which one of the following is a change that can always be handled by change management techniques?
    A.   Incremental change
    B.   Re-architecting change
    C.   Regulatory change
    D.   Simplification change

Q16: Complete the sentence: The process of managing architecture
      requirements applies to_____?
      A. All ADM phases
      B. The Preliminary Phase
      C. Phase A: Architecture Vision
      D. The Requirements Management phase

7.14 Recommended Reading

The following are recommended sources of further information for this
chapter:

- The TOGAF Standard, Version 9.2 Part II: ADM, Preliminary Phase
  through to ADM Architecture Requirements Management

Chapter 8

ADM Guidelines and Techniques

8.1 Key Learning Points

This chapter will help you understand the guidelines and techniques provided to support application of the TOGAF Architecture Development Method (ADM).

Key Points Explained

This chapter will help you to answer the following questions:

- What are the contents of Part III of the TOGAF standard?
- How to use the TOGAF ADM in the context of a specific architectural style?
- What is an Architecture Principle?
- Why are Architecture Principles needed and where are they used within the TOGAF ADM?
- What is a business scenario?
- What is the gap analysis technique?
- What does the TOGAF standard mean by interoperability?
- What is Business Transformation Readiness?
- What are the main characteristics of Risk Management?
- What is Capability-Based Planning?

8.2 ADM Guidelines and Techniques Overview

(Syllabus Reference: Unit 7, Learning Outcome 1: You should be able to briefly explain the contents of Part III, ADM Guidelines and Techniques.)

Part III: ADM Guidelines and Techniques contains a collection of guidelines and techniques for use in adapting and applying the TOGAF ADM. Additional guidelines and techniques are also in the TOGAF Library.

The guidelines document how to adapt the ADM process, whereas the techniques are used when applying the ADM process.

Guidelines for adapting the ADM process include:

- Ways to apply iteration to the ADM
- Applying the ADM at different levels of the enterprise
- How to use the TOGAF framework with different architectural styles

Syllabus Coverage for TOGAF Techniques

The TOGAF 9 Foundation Syllabus covers the following topics:

- Using the TOGAF ADM in the context of a specific Architectural Style
- Architecture Principles
- Stakeholder Management
- Architecture Patterns
- Business Scenarios
- Gap Analysis
- Migration Planning Techniques
- Interoperability Requirements
- Business Transformation Readiness Assessment
- Risk Management
- Capability-Based Planning

8.3 Using the TOGAF ADM in the Context of a Specific Architectural Style

(Syllabus Reference: Unit 7, Learning Outcome 16: You should be able to briefly explain the use of the TOGAF ADM in the context of a specific architectural style.)

The TOGAF framework is designed to be flexible and it can be readily adapted to a number of architectural styles.

When using the TOGAF standard to support a specific architectural style the practitioner must take into account the combination of distinctive features in which architecture is performed or expressed. As a first step, the distinctive features of a style must be identified.

For example, The Open Group definition for SOA identifies the following distinctive features:

- It is based on the design of the services – which mirror real-world business activities – comprising the enterprise (or inter-enterprise) business processes
- Service representation utilizes business descriptions to provide context (i.e., business process, goal, rule, policy, service interface, and service component) and implements services using service orchestration
- It places unique requirements on the infrastructure – it is recommended that implementations use open standards to realize interoperability and location transparency
- Implementations are environment-specific – they are constrained or enabled by context and must be described within that context

The second step is determining how these distinctive features will be addressed. Addressing a distinctive style should not call for significant changes to the TOGAF framework; instead it should adjust the models, viewpoints, and tools used by the practitioner.

In Phase B, Phase C, and Phase D the practitioner is expected to select the relevant architecture resources, including models, viewpoints, and tools, to properly describe the architecture domain and demonstrate that stakeholder concerns are addressed. Depending upon the distinctive features, different architectural styles will add new elements that must be described, highlight existing elements, adjust the notation used to describe the architecture, and focus the architect on some stakeholders or stakeholder concerns.

Addressing the distinctive features will usually include extensions to the Architecture Content Metamodel and the use of specific notation or modeling techniques and the identification of viewpoints. Whether the style is dominant will determine whether it is necessary to revisit the Preliminary Phase and make changes to the Architecture Capability or whether support for the distinctive feature is possible within the scope of selection expected within a single ADM cycle.

8.4 Architecture Principles

(Syllabus Reference: Unit 7, Learning Outcome 2: You should be able to briefly explain the need for Architecture Principles and where they are used within the TOGAF ADM.)

Architecture Principles are a set of general rules and guidelines for the architecture being developed.

They are intended to be enduring and seldom amended, and inform and support the way in which an organization sets about fulfilling its mission. Often they are one element of a structured set of ideas that collectively define and guide the organization, from values through to actions and results.

Principles are an initial output of the Preliminary Phase and are used throughout the ADM to provide a framework for guiding decision-making within the enterprise.

Depending on the organization, principles may be established within different domains and at different levels. Two key domains inform the development and utilization of architecture:

- **Enterprise Principles** provide a basis for decision-making throughout an enterprise and dictate how the organization fulfills its mission
  Such principles are commonly used as a means of harmonizing decision-making. They are a key element in a successful Architecture Governance strategy. Within the broad domain of enterprise principles, it is common to have subsidiary principles within a business or organizational unit; for example IT, HR, domestic operations, or overseas operations.
- **Architecture Principles** are a set of principles that relate to architecture work
  They reflect consensus across the enterprise, and embody the spirit of the Enterprise Architecture. Architecture Principles govern the architecture process, affecting the development, maintenance, and use of the Enterprise Architecture.

Part III: ADM Guidelines and Techniques contains guidelines for developing principles and a detailed set of generic Architecture Principles.

8.4.1 The TOGAF Template for Defining Architecture Principles

(Syllabus Reference: Unit 7, Learning Outcome 3: You should be able to describe the standard template for Architecture Principles.)

The TOGAF standard defines a recommended way of describing principles, as shown in Table 10. In addition to a definition statement, each principle should have associated rationale and implication statements, both to promote understanding and acceptance of the principles themselves, and to support the use of the principles in explaining and justifying why specific decisions are made.

Table 10:   TOGAF Template for Defining Principles

Section	Description
Name	Should represent both the essence of the rule and be easy to remember. Specific technology platforms should not be mentioned in the name or statement of a principle. Avoid ambiguous words in the name and in the statement such as: "support", "open", "consider", and for lack of good measure the word "avoid", itself, be careful with "manage(ment)", and look for unnecessary adjectives and adverbs.
Statement	Should succinctly and unambiguously communicate the fundamental rule. For the most part, the principle's statements for managing information are similar among organizations. It is vital that the statement be unambiguous.
Rationale	Should highlight the business benefits of adhering to the principle, using business terminology. Point to the similarity of information and technology principles to the principles governing business operations. Also describe the relationship to other principles, and the intentions regarding a balanced interpretation. Describe situations where one principle would be given precedence or carry more weight than another for making a decision.
Implications	Should highlight the requirements, both for the business and IT, for carrying out the principle – in terms of resources, costs, and activities/tasks. It will often be apparent that current systems, standards, or practices would be incongruent with the principle upon adoption. The impact on the business and consequences of adopting a principle should be clearly stated. The reader should readily discern the answer to: "How does this affect me?" It is important not to oversimplify, trivialize, or judge the merit of the impact. Some of the implications will be identified as potential impacts only, and may be speculative rather than fully analyzed.

Example 1:   Simple Principle

Self-Serve	
Statement	Customers should be able to serve themselves.
Rationale	Applying this principle will improve customer satisfaction, reduce administrative overhead, and potentially improve revenue.
Implications	There is an implication to improve ease-of-use and minimize training needs; for example, members should be able to update their contact details, etc. and be able to buy additional membership products online.

8.4.2   What Makes a Good Architecture Principle?

(Syllabus Reference: Unit 7, Learning Outcome 4: You should be able to explain what makes a good Architecture Principle.)

There are five criteria that distinguish a good set of principles, as shown in Table 11.

Table 11:   Recommended Criteria for Quality Principles

Criteria	Description
Understandability	The underlying tenets of a principle can be quickly grasped and understood by individuals throughout the organization. The intention of the principle is clear and unambiguous, so that violations, whether intentional or not, are minimized.
Robustness	Principles should enable good quality decisions about architectures and plans to be made, and enforceable policies and standards to be created. Each principle should be sufficiently definitive and precise to support consistent decision-making in complex, potentially controversial situations.
Completeness	Every potentially important principle governing the management of information and technology for the organization is defined. The principles cover every situation perceived.
Consistency	Strict adherence to one principle may require a loose interpretation of another principle. The set of principles must be expressed in a way that allows a balance of interpretations. Principles should not be contradictory to the point where adhering to one principle would violate the spirit of another. Every word in a principle statement should be carefully chosen to allow consistent yet flexible interpretation.
Stability	Principles should be enduring, yet able to accommodate changes. An amendment process should be established for adding, removing, or altering principles after they are ratified initially.

8.5 Business Scenarios

The business scenarios technique is described in the TOGAF® Series Guide: Business Scenarios.

8.5.1 What is a Business Scenario?

(Syllabus Reference: Unit 7, Learning Outcome 5: You should understand what a business scenario is and its purpose.)

A key factor in the success of any other major project is the extent to which it is linked to business requirements, and demonstrably supports and enables the enterprise to achieve its business objectives. Business scenarios are a technique used to help identify and understand the business requirements that an architecture must address.

A business scenario describes:
- A business process, application, or set of applications
- The business and technology environment
- The people and computing components ("actors") who execute the scenario
- The desired outcome of proper execution

The technique may be used iteratively, at different levels of detail in the hierarchical decomposition of the Business Architecture. The generic business scenario process is as follows:
- Identify, document, and rank the problem that is driving the project
- Document, as high-level architecture models, the business and technical environments where the problem situation is occurring
- Identify and document desired objectives; the results of handling the problems successfully
- Identify human actors and their place in the business model, the human participants, and their roles
- Identify computer actors and their place in the technology model, the computing elements, and their roles
- Identify and document roles, responsibilities, and measures of success per actor, the required scripts per actor, and the desired results of handling the situation properly

- Check for fitness-for-purpose of inspiring subsequent architecture work, and refine only if necessary

This is also summarized in Figure 16.

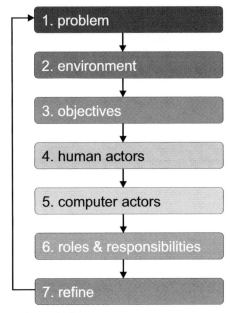

Figure 16:   The Business Scenario Process

A good business scenario represents a significant business need or problem, and enables vendors to understand the value of a solution to the customer. A good business scenario is also "SMART":

- Specific, by defining what needs to be done
- Measurable, through clear metrics for success
- Actionable, by clearly segmenting the problem and providing the basis for a solution
- Realistic, in that the problem can be solved within the bounds of physical reality, time, and cost constraints
- Time-bound, in that there is a clear statement of when the opportunity expires

8.5.2 The Use of Business Scenarios in the ADM

(Syllabus Reference: Unit 7, Learning Outcome 6: You should be able to explain where business scenarios are used within the ADM cycle.)

Business scenarios figure most prominently in the initial phase of an ADM cycle, Architecture Vision, when they are used to define relevant business requirements, and to build consensus with business management and other stakeholders.

They may also be used in other phases, particularly during Business Architecture, to derive the characteristics of the architecture directly from the high-level requirements of the business.

Because business requirements are important throughout all phases of the ADM cycle, the business scenarios technique has an important role to play in the TOGAF ADM, by ensuring that the business requirements themselves are complete and correct.

8.6 Gap Analysis

(Syllabus Reference: Unit 7, Learning Outcome 7: You should be able to explain the purpose of gap analysis.)

The technique known as gap analysis is widely used in the ADM to validate an architecture that is being developed. A key step in validating an architecture is to consider what may have been forgotten. The architecture must support all of the essential information processing needs of the organization. The most critical source of gaps that should be considered is stakeholder concerns that have not been addressed in prior architectural work.

The basic premise is to highlight a shortfall between the Baseline Architecture and the Target Architecture; that is, items that have been deliberately omitted, accidentally left out, or not yet defined.

Potential sources of gaps include:
- Business domain gaps:
  - People gaps (e.g., cross-training requirements)
  - Process gaps (e.g., process inefficiencies)
  - Tools gaps (e.g., duplicate or missing tool functionality)
  - Information gaps
  - Measurement gaps

- — Financial gaps
- — Facilities gaps (buildings, office space, etc.)
- Data domain gaps:
  - — Data not of sufficient currency
  - — Data not located where it is needed
  - — Not the data that is needed
  - — Data not available when needed
  - — Data not created
  - — Data not consumed
  - — Data relationship gaps
- Applications impacted, eliminated, or created
- Technologies impacted, eliminated, or created

(Syllabus Reference: Unit 7, Learning Outcome 8: You should be able to describe the gap analysis technique.)

The steps are as follows:
- Draw up a matrix with all the Architecture Building Blocks (ABBs) of the Baseline Architecture on the vertical axis, and all the ABBs of the Target Architecture on the horizontal axis
- Add to the Baseline Architecture axis a final row labeled "New ABBs", and to the Target Architecture axis a final column labeled "Eliminated ABBs"
- Where an ABB is available in both the Baseline and Target Architectures, record this with "Included" at the intersecting cell
- Where an ABB from the Baseline Architecture is missing in the Target Architecture, each must be reviewed
  If it was correctly eliminated, mark it as such in the appropriate "Eliminated" cell. If it was not, you have uncovered an accidental omission in your Target Architecture that must be addressed by reinstating the ABB in the next iteration of the architecture design – mark it as such in the appropriate "Eliminated" cell.
- Where an ABB from the Target Architecture cannot be found in the Baseline Architecture, mark it at the intersection with the "New" row as a gap that needs to filled, either by developing or procuring the building block

When the exercise is complete, anything under "Eliminated Services" or "New Services" is a gap, which should either be explained as correctly eliminated, or marked as to be addressed by reinstating or developing/procuring the function.

Table 12 shows examples of gaps between the Baseline Architecture and the Target Architecture; in this case the missing elements are "broadcast services" and "shared screen services".

Table 12:   Gap Analysis Example

Target Architecture → Baseline Architecture ↓	Video Conferencing Services	Enhanced Telephony Services	Mailing List Services	Eliminated Services ↓
Broadcast Services				Intentionally Eliminated
Video Conferencing Services	Included			
Enhanced Telephony Services		Potential Match		
Shared Screen Services				Unintentionally excluded – a gap in Target Architecture
New →		Gap: Enhanced services to be developed or produced	Gap: Enhanced services to be developed or produced	

The gap analysis technique should be used in Phases B, C, D, and E of the ADM.

8.7 Interoperability

(Syllabus Reference: Unit 7, Learning Outcome 9: You should be able to explain the term interoperability.)

The TOGAF standard defines interoperability as "the ability to share information and services". Defining the degree to which information and services are to be shared is very important, especially in a complex organization and/or extended enterprise.

Many organizations find it useful to categorize interoperability as follows:
- **Operational or Business Interoperability** defines how business processes are to be shared
- **Information Interoperability** defines how information is to be shared
- **Technical Interoperability** defines how technical services are to be shared or at least connect to one another

From an IT perspective, it is also useful to consider interoperability in a similar vein to Enterprise Application Integration (EAI); specifically:
- **Presentation Integration/Interoperability** is where a common look-and-feel approach through a common portal-like solution guides the user to the underlying functionality of the set of systems
- **Information Integration/Interoperability** is where the corporate information is seamlessly shared between the various corporate applications to achieve, for example, a common set of client information
  Normally this is based upon a commonly accepted corporate ontology and shared services for the structure, quality, access, and security/privacy for the information.
- **Application Integration/Interoperability** is where the corporate functionality is integrated and shareable so that the applications are not duplicated (e.g., one change of address service/component; not one for every application) and are seamlessly linked together through functionality such as workflow
  This impacts the business and infrastructure applications and is very closely linked to corporate business process unification/interoperability.
- **Technical Integration/Interoperability** includes common methods and shared services for the communication, storage, processing, and access to data primarily in the application platform and communications infrastructure domains
  This interoperability is premised upon the degree of rationalization of the corporate IT infrastructure, based upon standards and/or common IT platforms. For example, multiple applications sharing one infrastructure or 10,000 corporate websites using one centralized content management/

web server (rather than thousands of servers and webmasters spread throughout the country/globe).

Example 2:   Example Interoperability Model

Example Interoperability Model
An example interoperability model from the Canadian Government follows. This model includes a high-level definition of three classes of interoperability and the nature of the information and services shared at each level. Interoperability is coined in terms of e-enablers for e-Government. The interoperability breakdown is as follows: <ul><li>Information interoperability:<ul><li>— Knowledge management</li><li>— Business intelligence</li><li>— Information management</li><li>— Trusted identity</li></ul></li><li>Business interoperability:<ul><li>— Delivery networks</li><li>— e-Democracy</li><li>— e-Business</li><li>— Enterprise resource management</li><li>— Relationship and case management</li></ul></li><li>Technical interoperability:<ul><li>— IT infrastructure</li></ul></li></ul>

8.7.1 Interoperability and the ADM

(Syllabus Reference: Unit 7, Learning Outcome 10: You should understand where interoperability requirements are used within the ADM.)

The determination of interoperability occurs throughout the ADM:

- In Phase A: Architecture Vision, the nature and security considerations of information and service exchanges are found using business scenarios
- In Phase B: Business Architecture, information and service exchanges are defined in business terms
- In Phase C: Data Architecture, the content of information exchanges is detailed using the corporate data and/or information exchange model
- In Phase C: Application Architecture, the ways that applications are to share information and services are specified

- In Phase D: Technology Architecture, appropriate technical mechanisms to permit information and service exchanges are specified
- In Phase E: Opportunities & Solutions, actual solutions are selected
- In Phase F: Migration Planning, interoperability is implemented logically

8.8 Business Transformation Readiness Assessment

(Syllabus Reference: Unit 7, Learning Outcome 11: You should understand Business Transformation Readiness Assessment.)

Enterprise Architecture often involves considerable change. Business Transformation Readiness Assessment provides a technique for understanding the readiness of an organization to accept change, identifying the issues, and dealing with them in the Implementation and Migration Plan.

(Syllabus Reference: Unit 7, Learning Outcome 12: You should understand where the Business Transformation Readiness Assessment technique is used within the ADM.)

Use of such a technique is key to a successful architecture transformation in Phases E and F. An initial assessment of business transformation readiness is carried out in Phase A.

This assessment is recommended to be a joint effort between corporate staff, lines of business, and IT planners.

The recommended activities are:
- Determine the readiness factors that will impact the organization
- Present the readiness factors using maturity models
- Assess the readiness factors, and determine the readiness factor ratings
- Assess the risks for each readiness factor and identify improvement actions to mitigate the risk
- Document the findings into the Capability Assessment and later incorporate the actions into the Implementation and Migration Plan in Phases E and F

8.9 Risk Management

(Syllabus Reference: Unit 7, Learning Outcome 13: You should understand the characteristics of Risk Management.)

Risk management is a technique used to mitigate risk when implementing an architecture project. There are two levels of risk that should be considered:

- Initial Level of Risk: Risk categorization prior to determining and implementing mitigating actions.
- Residual Level of Risk: Risk categorization after implementation of mitigating actions.

The recommended process for managing risk consists of the following activities:

- Risk classification
- Risk identification
- Initial risk assessment
- Risk mitigation and residual risk assessment
- Risk monitoring

8.9.1 Risk Management in the ADM

(Syllabus Reference: Unit 7, Learning Outcome 14: You should understand where risk management is used within the TOGAF ADM.)

Risk is pervasive in any Enterprise Architecture activity and present in all phases within the ADM. Identification of business transformation risks and mitigation activities is first determined in Phase A as part of the initial Business Transformation Readiness Assessment. It is recommended that risk mitigation activities be included within the Statement of Architecture Work.

The risk identification and mitigation assessment worksheets are maintained as governance artifacts and are kept up-to-date in Phase G (Implementation Governance) where risk monitoring is conducted.

Implementation governance can identify critical risks that are not being mitigated and might require another full or partial ADM cycle.

8.10 Capability-Based Planning

*(Syllabus Reference: Unit 7, Learning Outcome 15: You should understand
Capability-Based Planning.)*

Capability-Based Planning is a business planning technique that focuses
on business outcomes. It is business-driven and business-led and combines
the requisite efforts of all lines of business to achieve the desired capability.
It accommodates most, if not all, of the corporate business models and is
especially useful in organizations where a latent capability to respond (e.g.,
an emergency preparedness unit) is required and the same resources are
involved in multiple capabilities. Often the need for these capabilities is
discovered and refined using business scenarios.

Figure 17 illustrates the relationship between Capability-Based Planning,
Enterprise Architecture, and portfolio/project management.

Figure 17:   Relationship between Capabilities, Enterprise Architecture, and Projects

8.11 Summary

This chapter has introduced a number of key guidelines and techniques that
are used to support application of the ADM. This has included:

- Understanding the contents of Part III of the TOGAF standard
- The use of Architecture Principles, including what they are and why they
  are needed
- The business scenarios technique, including what it is and where it is used
  in the ADM
- The gap analysis technique and its purpose

- The term interoperability, categorizations of interoperability, and where interoperability requirements are used within the ADM
- The Business Transformation Readiness Assessment technique, including what it is and where it is used in the ADM
- The main characteristics of risk management, and where it is used in the ADM
- Capability-Based Planning

8.12 Test Yourself Questions

Q1: Which one of the following statements about Architecture Principles is *not* true?

A. They are a set of general rules for the architecture being developed.

B. They are intended to be enduring and seldom amended.

C. They are an initial output from the Preliminary Phase.

D. They are used in the Requirements Management phase to dispose of, address, and prioritize requirements.

Q2: Which part of the TOGAF template for defining Architecture Principles should highlight the business benefits of adhering to the principle?

A. Implications

B. Name

C. Rationale

D. Statement

Q3: A good business scenario should be "SMART". What does the letter "S" stand for?

A. Solution-oriented

B. Specific

C. Strategic

D. Stakeholder-oriented

Q4: Where is the business scenarios technique expected to be most used in the ADM cycle?

A. Preliminary Phase

B. Phase A: Architecture Vision

    C.   Phase F: Migration Planning

    D.   Phase H: Architecture Change Management

Q5. A gap analysis reveals that an Architecture Building Block that was present in the Baseline Architecture is missing in the Target Architecture. Which of the following does *not* apply?

    A.   A review should occur.

    B.   If the building block was correctly eliminated, it should be added to the Target Architecture in the next iteration.

    C.   If the building block was correctly eliminated, it should be marked as such in the "Eliminated" cell.

    D.   If the building block was incorrectly eliminated, it should be reinstated to the architecture design in the next iteration.

    E.   If the building block was incorrectly eliminated, it should be recorded as an accidental omission.

Q6. The TOGAF standard defines interoperability as "the ability to share information and services". Which of the following categories utilizes a common look-and-feel approach through a common portal-like solution to interact with the users?

    A.   Application interoperability

    B.   Information interoperability

    C.   Presentation interoperability

    D.   Technical interoperability

Q7. Which of the following best describes the Business Transformation Readiness Assessment technique?

    A.   A technique to define the degree to which information and services are to be shared

    B.   A technique used to identify and understand the business requirements an architecture must address

    C.   A technique used to develop general rules and guidelines for the architecture being developed

    D.   A technique used to understand the readiness of an organization to accept change

Q8.   Which of the following best describes the meaning of "Residual Level of Risk" in risk management?
   A.   The categorization prior to determining risks
   B.   The categorization after implementing mitigating actions
   C.   The categorization after the initial risk assessment
   D.   The categorization after risk identification

Q9.   Which of the following best describes the Capability-Based Planning technique?
   A.   A technique used to plan the degree to which information and services are to be shared
   B.   A technique used to validate an architecture
   C.   A technique used for business planning that focuses on business outcomes
   D.   A technique used to develop general rules and guidelines for the architecture being developed

8.13 Recommended Reading

The following are recommended sources of further information for this chapter:
- The TOGAF Standard, Version 9.2 Part III: ADM Guidelines and Techniques, Introduction to Part III
- The TOGAF Standard, Version 9.2 Part III: ADM Guidelines and Techniques, Architecture Principles
- TOGAF® Series Guide: Business Scenarios
- The TOGAF Standard, Version 9.2 Part III: ADM Guidelines and Techniques, Gap Analysis
- The TOGAF Standard, Version 9.2 Part III: ADM Guidelines and Techniques, Interoperability Requirements
- The TOGAF Standard, Version 9.2 Part III: ADM Guidelines and Techniques, Business Transformation Readiness Assessment
- The TOGAF Standard, Version 9.2 Part III: ADM Guidelines and Techniques, Risk Management
- The TOGAF Standard, Version 9.2 Part III: ADM Guidelines and Techniques, Capability-Based Planning

Chapter 9

Architecture Governance

9.1 Key Learning Points

This chapter will help you understand Architecture Governance, and how it contributes to the Architecture Development Cycle.

Key Points Explained

This chapter will help you to answer the following questions:

- What is Architecture Governance?
- What are the main concepts that make up an Architecture Governance Framework?
- Why is Architecture Governance beneficial?
- What is the need to establish an Architecture Board?
- What are the responsibilities of an Architecture Board?
- What is the role of Architecture Contracts?
- What is Architecture Compliance?
- How can the ADM be used to establish an Architecture Capability?

The TOGAF standard provides significant guidance on establishing effective Architecture Governance and coordinating with other governance processes within the organization. Effective governance ensures that problems are identified early and that subsequent changes to the environment occur in a controlled manner. [Source: Bill Estrem, "TOGAF to the Rescue" (www.opengroup.org/downloads)]

9.2 Introduction to Architecture Governance

(Syllabus Reference: Unit 8, Learning Outcome 1: You should be able to briefly explain the concept of Architecture Governance.)

Architecture Governance is the practice by which Enterprise Architectures and other architectures are managed and controlled at an enterprise-wide level.

Architecture Governance includes the following:
- Implementing a system of controls over the creation and monitoring of all architectural components and activities, to ensure the effective introduction, implementation, and evolution of architectures within the organization
- Implementing a system to ensure compliance with internal and external standards and regulatory obligations
- Establishing processes that support effective management of the above processes within agreed parameters
- Developing practices that ensure accountability to a clearly identified stakeholder community, both inside and outside the organization

Architecture Governance typically operates within a hierarchy of governance structures which, particularly in the larger enterprise, can include the following as distinct domains with their own disciplines and processes:
- Corporate Governance
- Technology Governance
- IT Governance
- Architecture Governance

Each of these domains of governance may exist at multiple geographic levels – global, regional, and local – within the overall enterprise. Corporate Governance is a broad topic and outside the scope of the TOGAF framework.

What is Governance?

Governance is about ensuring that business is conducted properly. It is less about overt control and strict adherence to rules, and more about effective usage of resources to ensure sustainability of an organization's strategic objectives.

The following characteristics, adapted from *Corporate Governance* (Naidoo, 2002[12]), are used in the TOGAF standard to highlight both the value and necessity for governance as an approach to be adopted within organizations and their dealings with all involved parties:

Discipline: All involved parties will have a commitment to adhere to procedures, processes, and authority structures established by the organization.

Transparency: All actions implemented and their decision support will be available for inspection by authorized organizations and provider parties.

Independence: All processes, decision-making, and mechanisms used will be established so as to minimize or avoid potential conflicts of interest.

Accountability: Identifiable groups within the organization – e.g., governance boards who take actions or make decisions – are authorized and accountable for their actions.

Responsibility: Each contracted party is required to act responsibly to the organization and its stakeholders.

Fairness: All decisions taken, processes used, and their implementation will not be allowed to create unfair advantage to any one particular party.

9.3 TOGAF Architecture Governance Framework

(Syllabus Reference: Unit 8, Learning Outcome 2: You should be able to describe the main concepts that make up an Architecture Governance Framework.)

Phase G of the TOGAF ADM is dedicated to Implementation Governance, which concerns itself with the realization of the architecture through change projects. Architecture Governance covers the management and control of all aspects of the development and evolution of architectures. It needs to be supported by an Architecture Governance Framework which assists in identifying effective processes so that the business responsibilities associated with Architecture Governance can be elucidated, communicated, and

---

11   Corporate Governance, Ranami Naidoo, Double Storey, 2002.

managed effectively. The TOGAF standard provides such a framework, which is described in the following sections.

9.3.1 Conceptual Structure

Architecture Governance is an approach, a series of processes, a cultural orientation, and set of owned responsibilities that ensure the integrity and effectiveness of the organization's architectures. The key concepts are shown in Figure 18.

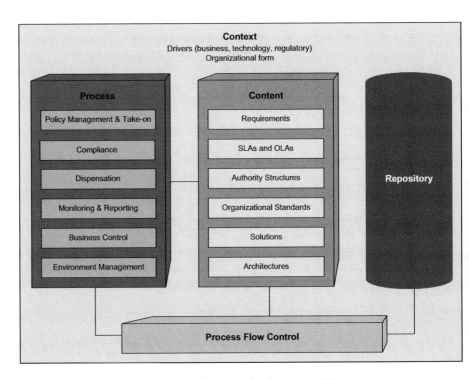

Figure 18:   Architecture Governance Framework – Conceptual Structure

The split of process, content, and context is key to supporting an Architecture Governance initiative. It allows the introduction of new governance material (for example, due to new regulations) without unduly impacting the processes. The content-agnostic approach ensures the framework is flexible.

Key Architecture Governance Processes

The following are the key processes:

- Policy Management and Take-On

- Compliance
- Dispensation
- Monitoring and Reporting
- Business Control
- Environment Management

9.3.2 Organizational Structure

Governance is the practice of managing and controlling architectures. An effective Architecture Governance structure requires processes, structures, and capabilities (see Figure 19) and will typically include a global governance board, local governance board, design authorities, and working parties.

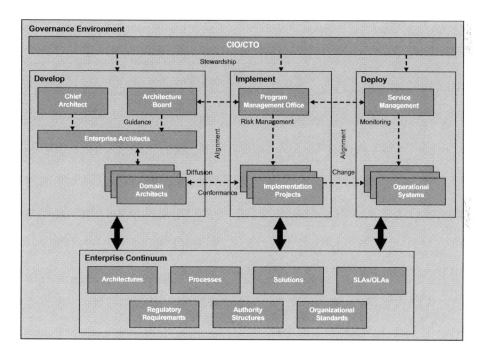

Figure 19:   Architecture Governance Framework – Organizational Structure

9.4 The Benefits of Architecture Governance

(Syllabus Reference: Unit 8, Learning Outcome 3: You should be able to explain why Architecture Governance is beneficial.)

Architecture Governance is beneficial because it:

- Links IT processes, resources, and information to organizational strategies and objectives
- Integrates and institutionalizes IT best practices
- Aligns with industry frameworks such as COBIT (planning and organizing, acquiring and implementing, delivering and supporting, and monitoring IT performance)
- Enables the organization to take full advantage of its information, infrastructure, and hardware/software assets
- Protects the underlying digital assets of the organization
- Supports regulatory and best practice requirements such as auditability, security, responsibility, and accountability
- Promotes visible risk management

What are the Key Success Factors when establishing Architecture Governance?

It is important to consider the following to ensure a successful approach to Architecture Governance, and effective management of the Architecture Contract:

- Establishment and operation of best practices for submission, adoption, re-use, reporting, and retirement of architecture policies, procedures, roles, skills, organizational structures, and support services
- Establishment of correct organizational responsibilities and structures to support Architecture Governance processes and reporting requirements
- Integration of tools and processes to facilitate take-up of processes (both procedural and cultural)
- Management of criteria for control of Architecture Governance processes, dispensations, compliance assessments, Service Level Agreements (SLAs), and Operational Level Agreements (OLAs)
- Meeting internal and external requirements for effectiveness, efficiency, confidentiality, integrity, availability, compliance, and reliability of Architecture Governance-related information, services, and processes

9.5 Architecture Board

(Syllabus Reference: Unit 8, Learning Outcome 4: You should be able to briefly explain the need for establishment of an Architecture Board.)

An Enterprise Architecture imposed without appropriate political backing is bound to fail. An important element in any Architecture Governance strategy is establishment of a cross-organizational Architecture Board to oversee the implementation of the governance strategy. This body should be representative of all the key stakeholders in the architecture, and will typically comprise a group of executives responsible for the review and maintenance of the overall architecture.

(Syllabus Reference: Unit 8, Learning Outcome 5: You should be able to list the responsibilities of an Architecture Board.)

The Architecture Board is typically made responsible, and accountable, for achieving some or all of the following goals:
- Providing the basis for all decision-making with regard to changes to the architectures
- Consistency between sub-architectures
- Establishing targets for re-use of components
- Flexibility of Enterprise Architecture; to meet business needs and utilize new technologies
- Enforcement of Architecture Compliance
- Improving the maturity level of architecture discipline within the organization
- Ensuring that the discipline of architecture-based development is adopted
- Supporting a visible escalation capability for out-of-bounds decisions

The Architecture Board is also responsible for operational items such as the monitoring and control of Architecture Contracts, and for governance items such as producing usable governance materials.

9.6 Architecture Contracts

(Syllabus Reference: Unit 8, Learning Outcome 6: You should be able to briefly explain the role of Architecture Contracts.)

Architecture Contracts are joint agreements between development partners and sponsors on the deliverables, quality, and fitness-for-purpose of an architecture. Successful implementation of these agreements will be delivered through effective Architecture Governance. Taking a governed approach to contract management ensures a system that continuously monitors integrity, changes, decision-making, and audit, as well as adherence to the principles, standards, and requirements of the enterprise. The architecture team may also be included in product procurement, to help minimize the opportunity for misinterpretation of the Enterprise Architecture.

9.7 Architecture Compliance

9.7.1 The Meaning of Architecture Compliance

(Syllabus Reference: Unit 8, Learning Outcome 7: You should be able to briefly explain the meaning of Architecture Compliance.)

The TOGAF standard defines the meaning of key terms such as "conformant", "compliant", etc. as shown in Figure 20.

Irrelevant:
The implementation has no features in common with the architecture specification (so the question of conformance does not arise).

Consistent:
The implementation has some features in common with the architecture specification, and those common features are implemented in accordance with the specification. However, some features in the architecture specification are not implemented, and the implementation has other features that are not covered by the specification.

Compliant:
Some features in the architecture specification are not implemented, but all features implemented are covered by the specification, and in accordance with it.

Conformant:
All the features in the architecture specification are implemented in accordance with the specification, but some more features are implemented that are not in accordance with it.

Fully Conformant:
There is full correspondence between architecture specification and implementation. All specified features are implemented in accordance with the specification, and there are no features implemented that are not covered by the specification.

Non-conformant:
Any of the above in which some features in the architecture specification are implemented not in accordance with the specification.

Figure 20:   Levels of Architecture Conformance

9.7.2 The Need for Architecture Compliance

(Syllabus Reference: Unit 8, Learning Outcome 8: You should be able to briefly explain the need for Architecture Compliance.)

Ensuring the compliance of individual projects within the Enterprise Architecture is an essential aspect of Architecture Governance. An Architecture Compliance strategy should be adopted. The TOGAF standard recommends two complementary processes:

- The Architecture function will be required to prepare a series of Project Architectures; i.e., project-specific views of the Enterprise Architecture that illustrate how the Enterprise Architecture impacts on the major projects within the organization (see ADM Phases A to F)
- The IT Governance function will define a formal Architecture Compliance Review process (see below) for reviewing the compliance of projects to the Enterprise Architecture

Apart from defining formal processes, the Architecture Governance function may also stipulate that the architecture function should extend beyond the role of architecture definition and standards selection, and participate also in the technology selection process, and even in the commercial relationships involved in external service provision and product purchases. This may help to minimize the opportunity for misinterpretation of the Enterprise Architecture, and maximize the value of centralized commercial negotiation.

9.7.3 The Purpose of Architecture Compliance Reviews

(Syllabus Reference: Unit 8, Learning Outcome 9: You should be able to briefly explain the purpose of Architecture Compliance Reviews.)

The purpose of an Architecture Compliance Review includes the following:

- To catch errors in the project architecture early, and thereby reduce the cost and risk of changes required later in the lifecycle; this in turn means that the overall project time is shortened, and that the business gets the bottom-line benefit of the architecture development faster
- To ensure the application of best practices to architecture work
- To provide an overview of the compliance of an architecture to mandated enterprise standards
- To identify where the standards themselves may require modification
- To identify services that are currently application-specific but might be provided as part of the enterprise infrastructure

- To document strategies for collaboration, resource sharing, and other synergies across multiple architecture teams
- To take advantage of advances in technology
- To communicate to management the status of technical readiness of the project
- To identify key criteria for procurement activities (e.g., for inclusion in Commercial Off-The-Shelf (COTS) product RFI/RFP documents)
- To identify and communicate significant architectural gaps to product and service providers

The Architecture Compliance Review can also be a good way of deciding between architectural alternatives, since the business decision-makers typically involved in the review can guide decisions in terms of what is best for the business, as opposed to what is technically more pleasing or elegant.

9.7.4 The Architecture Compliance Review Process

(Syllabus Reference: Unit 8, Learning Outcome 10: You should be able to briefly describe the Architecture Compliance Review process.)

An Architecture Compliance Review is a scrutiny of the compliance of a specific project against established architectural criteria, spirit, and business objectives. The TOGAF standard describes a process, including the roles and actions to undertake a review and deliver an assessment report, as summarized in Figure 21.

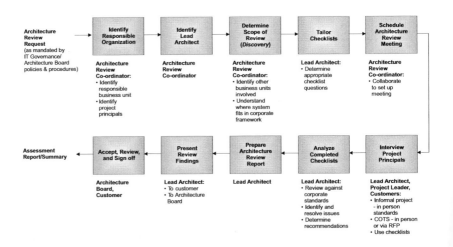

Figure 21:   Architecture Compliance Review Process

This consists of 12 steps as follows:

Step	Action	Notes	Who
1	Request Architecture Review	Mandated by governance policies	Anyone with an interest in or responsibility for the business area
2	Identify responsible part of organization and project principals		Architecture Review Co-ordinator
3	Identify Lead Enterprise Architect and other architects		Architecture Review Co-ordinator
4	Determine scope of review	Identify which other business units/departments are involved Understand where the system fits into the corporate architecture framework	Architecture Review Co-ordinator
5	Tailor checklists	To address the business requirements	Lead Enterprise Architect
6	Schedule Architecture Review meeting		Architecture Review Co-ordinator with collaboration of Lead Enterprise Architect
7	Interview project principals	To get background and technical information For internal project: in person For COTS: in person or via RFP Use checklists	Lead Enterprise Architect, and/ or Architect, Project Leader, and Customers
8	Analyze completed checklists	Review against corporate standards Identify and resolve issues Determine recommendations	Lead Enterprise Architect
9	Prepare Architecture Compliance Review report	May involve supporting staff	Lead Enterprise Architect
10	Present review findings	To Customer To Architecture Board	Lead Enterprise Architect

Step	Action	Notes	Who
11	Accept review and sign-off		Architecture Board and Customer
12	Send assessment report/ summary to Architecture Review Co-ordinator		Lead Enterprise Architect

9.8 Using the ADM to Establish an Architecture Capability

(Syllabus Reference: Unit 8, Learning Outcome 11: You should be able to briefly explain how the ADM can be used to establish an Architecture Capability.)

Establishing a sustainable Architecture Capability within an organization can be achieved by adhering to the same approach that is used to establish any other capability – such as a business process management capability – within an organization. The ADM is an ideal method to be used to architect and govern the implementation of such a capability. Applying the ADM with the specific Architecture Vision to establish an architecture practice within the organization would achieve this objective.

The TOGAF standard states that this should not be seen as a phase of an architecture project, or a one-off project, but rather as an ongoing practice that provides the context, environment, and resources to govern and enable architecture delivery to the organization. As an architecture project is executed within this environment it might request a change to the architecture practice that would trigger another cycle of the ADM to extend the architecture practice.

Implementing any capability within an organization would require the design of the four domain architectures: Business, Data, Application, and Technology. Establishing the architecture practice within an organization would therefore require the design of:

- The Business Architecture of the architecture practice that will highlight the Architecture Governance, architecture processes, architecture organizational structure, architecture information requirements, architecture products, etc.

- The Data Architecture that would define the structure of the organization's Enterprise Continuum and Architecture Repository
- The Application Architecture specifying the functionality and/or applications services required to enable the architecture practice
- The Technology Architecture that depicts the architecture practice's infrastructure requirements and deployment in support of the architecture applications and Enterprise Continuum

9.9 Summary

Architecture Governance is the practice and orientation by which Enterprise Architectures and other architectures are managed and controlled at an enterprise-wide level. It includes the following:

- Implementing a system of controls over the creation and monitoring of all architecture components and activities, to ensure the effective introduction, implementation, and evolution of architectures within the organization
- Implementing a system to ensure compliance with internal and external standards and regulatory obligations
- Establishing processes that support effective management of the above processes within agreed parameters
- Developing practices that ensure accountability to a clearly identified stakeholder community, both inside and outside the organization

An important element in any Architecture Governance strategy is establishment of a cross-organizational Architecture Board to oversee the implementation of the governance strategy. This body should be representative of all the key stakeholders in the architecture, and will typically comprise a group of executives responsible for the review and maintenance of the overall architecture.

Architecture Contracts are joint agreements between development partners and sponsors on the deliverables, quality, and fitness-for-purpose of an architecture. Successful implementation of these agreements will be delivered through effective Architecture Governance.

Ensuring the compliance of individual projects within the Enterprise Architecture is an essential aspect of Architecture Governance. An Architecture Compliance strategy should be adopted.

9.10 Test Yourself Questions

Q1:   Which of the following statements about Architecture Governance is *not* correct?

A.   It is the practice and orientation by which Enterprise Architectures and other architectures are managed and controlled.

B.   The Chief Architect manages the Architecture Governance activity.

C.   An Architecture Governance Framework supports it.

D.   It is a set of owned responsibilities that ensure the integrity and effectiveness of the organization's architecture.

Q2:   Complete the sentence: The following are included in Architecture Governance, *except*:

A.   Implementing a system of controls over expenditure within the enterprise

B.   Implementing a system of controls over the creation and monitoring of all architecture components and activities

C.   Establishing processes that support effective management of the Architecture Governance process

D.   Developing practices that ensure accountability to stakeholders

Q3:   Which of the following maps to the characteristic "transparency"?

A.   All decisions taken, processes used, and their implementation will not be allowed to create unfair advantage to any one particular party.

B.   Each contractual party is required to act responsibly to the organization and its shareholders.

C.   All actions implemented and their decision support will be available for inspection by authorized organizations and provider parties.

D.   All involved parties will have a commitment to adhere to procedures, processes, and authority structures established by the organization.

E. All processes, decision-making, and mechanisms used will be established so as to minimize or avoid potential conflicts of interest.

Q4: Conceptually, the structure of an Architecture Governance Framework consists of process, content, and context (stored in the repository). Which one of the following is *not* included in content:
A. Compliance
B. SLAs and OLAs
C. Organizational standards
D. Regulatory requirements
E. Architectures

Q5: Complete the sentence: All of the following are key Architecture Governance processes, *except*:
A. Compliance
B. Dispensation
C. Monitoring and reporting
D. Budgetary control
E. Business control

Q6: Why is Architecture Governance beneficial?
A. It links IT processes, resources, and information to organizational strategies and objectives.
B. It integrates and institutionalizes IT best practices.
C. It enables the organization to take full advantage of its information, infrastructure, and hardware/software assets.
D. It protects the underlying digital assets of the organization.
E. All of these.

Q7: Which one of the following is *not* the responsibility of an Architecture Board?
A. Resourcing of architecture projects
B. Decision-making with regard to changes to the architectures
C. Enforcement of Architecture Compliance
D. Monitoring of Architecture Contracts

Q8: Which one of the following best describes an Architecture Contract?
    A. An agreement between the development partners and stakeholders on the acceptable risks and mitigating actions for an architecture
    B. An agreement between development partners and sponsors on the deliverables, quality, and fitness-for-purpose of an architecture
    C. An agreement between the lead architect and the development partners on the enforcement of Architecture Compliance for an architecture
    D. An agreement between development partners and sponsors on how best to monitor implementation of the architecture

Q9: The TOGAF standard defines a set of terms to describe Architecture Compliance. Which one of the following applies to the case where an implementation has no features in common with the architecture specification?
    A. Compliant
    B. Conformant
    C. Irrelevant
    D. Non-conformant

Q10: In an Architecture Compliance Review, who is responsible for accepting and signing off on the review?
    A. Architecture Board
    B. Architecture Review Co-ordinator
    C. Lead Enterprise Architect
    D. Project Leader

Q11: When using the ADM to establish an Architecture Capability, which phase would define the infrastructure requirements to support the practice?
    A. Application Architecture
    B. Business Architecture
    C. Data Architecture
    D. Technology Architecture

9.11 Recommended Reading

The following are recommended sources of further information for this chapter:

- The TOGAF Standard, Version 9.2 Part VI: Architecture Capability Framework, Establishing an Architecture Capability
- The TOGAF Standard, Version 9.2 Part VI: Architecture Capability Framework, Architecture Board
- The TOGAF Standard, Version 9.2 Part VI: Architecture Capability Framework, Architecture Compliance
- The TOGAF Standard, Version 9.2 Part VI: Architecture Capability Framework, Architecture Contracts
- The TOGAF Standard, Version 9.2 Part VI: Architecture Capability Framework, Architecture Governance

Chapter 10

Architecture Views, Architecture Viewpoints, and Stakeholders

10.1 Key Learning Points

This chapter will help you understand the concepts of architecture views and architecture viewpoints, and their role in communicating with stakeholders.

Key Points Explained

This chapter will help you to answer the following questions:

- What are the key concepts for architecture views and architecture viewpoints in the TOGAF standard?
- How can a simple example of an architecture viewpoint and architecture view be described?
- What are the relationships between stakeholders, concerns, architecture views, and architecture viewpoints?
- How are architecture views created?

10.2 Concepts and Definitions

(Syllabus Reference: Unit 9, Learning Outcome 1: You should be able to define and explain the following concepts: stakeholders, concerns, architecture views, and architecture viewpoints.)

In this section we introduce the following concepts and definitions:

- System
- Stakeholders
- Concerns
- Architecture Views
- Architecture Viewpoints

These have been adapted from more formal definitions in ISO/IEC/IEEE 42010:2011. Many people use these terms in different ways. Here we need to understand them within the context of the TOGAF standard.

10.2.1 System

A *system* is a combination of interacting elements organized to achieve one or more stated purposes.

[Source: ISO/IEC/IEEE 15288:2015]

"The term *system* encompasses individual applications, systems in the traditional sense, subsystems, systems of systems, product lines, product families, whole enterprises, and other aggregations of interest."

[Source: ISO/IEC/IEEE 42010:2011]

10.2.2 Stakeholders

Stakeholders are individuals, teams, organizations, or classes thereof, having an interest in a system. They are people who have key roles in, or *concerns* about, the system; for example, users, developers, etc.

A system has one or more stakeholders. Each stakeholder typically has interests in, or concerns relative to, that system. Figure 22 shows a typical set of stakeholders for an Enterprise Architecture, with defined categories of stakeholder type.

Figure 22:   A Typical Set of Stakeholders for an Enterprise Architecture

10.2.3 Concerns

Concerns are interests in a system relevant to one or more of its stakeholders. Concerns may pertain to any aspect of the system's functioning, development, or operation, including considerations such as performance, reliability, security, distribution, and evolvability and may determine the acceptability of the system. For example, a Security Architect could have the following concerns: authentication, authorization, audit, assurance, availability, asset protection, administration, risk management.

> The terms "concern" and "requirement" are not synonymous. A concern is an area of interest.
> Concerns are the root of the process of decomposition into requirements.
> Concerns are represented in the architecture by these requirements. Requirements should be SMART (i.e., should include specific metrics).
> [Source: The TOGAF Standard, Version 9.2 Part IV: Architecture Content Framework, Architectural Artifacts]

10.2.4 Architecture View

An *architecture view* (synonym: view) is a representation of a system from the perspective of a related set of concerns. An architecture view is what you see (or what a stakeholder sees).

An architect creates architecture models. An architecture view consists of parts of these, chosen to show stakeholders that their concerns are being met. For example, just as a building architect will create wiring diagrams, floor plans, and elevations to describe different facets of a building to its different stakeholders (electricians, owners, planning officials), so an Enterprise Architect must create different architecture views of the business, information system, and technical architecture for the stakeholders who have concerns related to these aspects. These might include business process, physical layout, and security views of an IT system.

Figure 23:   Typical (Architecture) Views from Building Architecture

10.2.5 Architecture Viewpoint

An *architecture viewpoint* (synonym: viewpoint) is the specification of the conventions for a particular kind of architecture view. It establishes the conventions for constructing, interpreting, and using an architecture view to address a specific concern (or set of concerns) about a system-of-interest. It effectively defines the perspective from which an architecture view is taken.

It defines how to construct and use an architecture view, the information needed, the modeling techniques for expressing and analyzing it, and a rationale for these choices (e.g., by describing the purpose and intended audience of the view).

The relationship between an architecture viewpoint and an architecture view is analogous to that of a template and an instance of the completed template. In constructing an Enterprise Architecture, an architect first selects the architecture viewpoints (templates), then constructs a set of corresponding architecture views (instances).

10.3 Architecture Views and Viewpoints

(Syllabus Reference: Unit 9, Learning Outcome 2: You should be able to describe a simple example of an architecture viewpoint and view.)

The architect uses architecture views and architecture viewpoints in the ADM cycle during Phases A through D for developing architectures for each domain (Business, Data, Application, and Technology).

Architecture Views and Architecture Viewpoints

An "architecture view" is what you see. An "architecture viewpoint" is where you are looking from; the vantage point or perspective that determines what you see (an architecture viewpoint can also be thought of as a schema).

Architecture viewpoints are generic, and can be stored in libraries for re-use, known as a viewpoint library.

An architecture view is always specific to the architecture for which it is created. Every architecture view has an associated architecture viewpoint that describes it, at least implicitly.

To illustrate the concepts of architecture views and architecture viewpoints, consider Example 3. This is a very simple airport system with two different stakeholders: the pilot and the air traffic controller. In this example we have abbreviated the terms to view and viewpoint.

Example 3:   Views and Viewpoints for a Simple Airport System

Views and Viewpoints for a Simple Airport System

The pilot has one view of the system, and the air traffic controller has another. Neither view represents the whole system, because the perspective of each stakeholder constrains (and reduces) how each sees the overall system.

The view of the pilot comprises some elements not viewed by the controller, such as passengers and fuel, while the view of the controller comprises some elements not viewed by the pilot, such as other planes. There are also elements shared between the views, such as the communication model between the pilot and the controller, and the vital information about the plane itself.

A viewpoint is a model (or description) of the information contained in a view. In this example, one viewpoint is the description of how the pilot sees the system, and the other viewpoint is how the controller sees the system. Pilots describe the system from their perspective, using a model of their position and vector toward or away from the runway. All pilots use this model, and the model has a specific language that is used to capture information and populate the model. Controllers describe the system differently, using a model of the airspace and the locations and vectors of aircraft within the airspace. Again, all controllers use a common language derived from the common model in order to capture and communicate information pertinent to their viewpoint.

> Fortunately, when controllers talk with pilots, they use a common communication language. (In other words, the models representing their individual viewpoints partially intersect.) Part of this common language is about location and vectors of aircraft, and is essential to safety. So in essence each viewpoint is an abstract model of how all the stakeholders of a particular type – all pilots, or all controllers – view the airport system. The interface to the human user of a tool is typically close to the model and language associated with the viewpoint. The unique tools of the pilot are fuel, altitude, speed, and location indicators. The main tool of the controller is radar. The common tool is a radio.

To summarize from Example 3, we can see that a view can subset the system through the perspective of the stakeholder, such as the pilot *versus* the controller. This subset can be described by an abstract model called a viewpoint, such as an air flight *versus* an air space model. This description of the view is documented in a partially specialized language, such as "pilot-speak" *versus* "controller-speak". Tools are used to assist the stakeholders, and they interface with each other in terms of the language derived from the viewpoint. When stakeholders use common tools, such as the radio contact between pilot and controller, a common language is essential.

For many architectures, a useful architecture viewpoint is that of business domains, which can be illustrated by an example from The Open Group.

The architecture viewpoint can be specified as follows:

Architecture Viewpoint Element	Description
Stakeholders	Management Board, Chief Executive Officer
Concerns	Show the top-level relationships between US/UK geographical sites and business functions.
Modeling technique	Nested boxes diagram Outer boxes = locations; inner boxes = business functions Semantics of nesting = functions performed in the locations

The corresponding view of The Open Group (in 2018) is shown in Figure 24.

Figure 24:   Example View – The Open Group Business Domains in the US/UK

10.4 The Relationship between Stakeholders, Concerns, Views, and Viewpoints

(Syllabus Reference: Unit 9, Learning Outcome 3: You should be able to discuss the relationship between stakeholders, concerns, architecture views, and architecture viewpoints.)

The relationship between stakeholders, concerns, architecture views, and architecture viewpoints are summarized in Figure 25.[12]

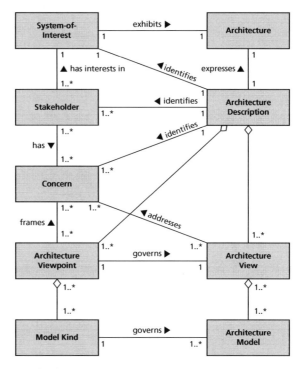

Figure 25:   Relationship between Basic Architectural Concepts

10.5 The Architecture View Creation Process

(Syllabus Reference: Unit 9, Learning Outcome 4: You should be able to describe the architecture view creation process.)

Architecture views are representations of the overall architecture in terms meaningful to stakeholders. They enable the architecture to be communicated to and understood by the stakeholders, so they can verify that the system will address their concerns.

---

12   Reprinted with permission from Figure 2 of ISO/IEC/IEEE 42010: 2011, Systems and Software Engineering — Architecture Description, with permission from IEEE. Copyright © 2011, by IEEE. The IEEE disclaims any responsibility or liability resulting from the placement and use in the described manner.

The architect chooses and develops a set of architecture views in the ADM cycle during Phases A through D that enable the architecture to be communicated to, and understood by, all the stakeholders, and enable them to verify that the system will address their concerns.

The choice of which particular architecture views to develop is one of the key decisions that the architect has to make.
The architect has a responsibility for ensuring:
- The completeness of the architecture:
  - Does it address all the concerns of its stakeholders?
- The integrity of the architecture:
  - Can the views be connected to each other?
  - Can the conflicting concerns be reconciled?
  - What trade-offs have been made (e.g., between security and performance)?

Recommended Steps
The following are the recommended steps to create the required views for a particular architecture:
- Refer to any existing libraries of architecture viewpoints
- Select key stakeholders
- Analyze their concerns and document them
- Select appropriate architecture viewpoints (based on the stakeholders and their concerns)
- Generate views of the system using the selected architecture viewpoints as templates

10.6 **Summary**
The TOGAF standard embraces the concepts and definitions of ISO/IEC/ IEEE 42010:2011, specifically those that guide the development of an architecture view, and make the view actionable, such as:
- Selecting key stakeholders
- Analyzing their concerns and documenting them
- Understanding how to model and deal with those concerns

The language used to depict the view is the architecture viewpoint. The viewpoints provided should be customized to create a set of architecture views that ensure all stakeholder concerns are met.

10.7 Test Yourself Questions

Q1:   Which of the following terms does the TOGAF standard use to describe people who have key roles in, or concerns about, a system?

   A.   Architect
   B.   Customer
   C.   Sponsor
   D.   Stakeholder

Q2:   Which of the following statements is *not* correct?

   A.   An architecture view can be thought of as a template for an architecture viewpoint.
   B.   An architecture viewpoint defines the perspective from which an architecture view is taken.
   C.   An architecture viewpoint defines how to construct and use an architecture view.
   D.   An architecture view is what a stakeholder sees.
   E.   An architecture view might describe business process for an IT system.

Q3:   Which of the following statements is *not* correct?

   A.   A concern might include performance and reliability.
   B.   A concern is an area of interest.
   C.   Concerns are key interests of the stakeholders.
   D.   Concern and requirement are synonymous.

Q4:   Which of the following statements describing relationships between stakeholders, concerns, views, and viewpoints is correct?

   A.   A concern is important to only one stakeholder.
   B.   A stakeholder identifies one or more concerns.
   C.   A viewpoint covers one concern.
   D.   A viewpoint consists of one or more views.

10.8 Recommended Reading

The following are recommended sources of further information for this chapter:

- The TOGAF Standard, Version 9.2 Part IV: Architecture Content Framework, Architectural Artifacts

Chapter 11

Building Blocks

11.1 Key Learning Points

This chapter will help you understand the concept of building blocks within the TOGAF standard.

Key Points Explained

This chapter will help you to answer the following questions:

- What is a building block?
- What is the difference between an Architecture Building Block and a Solution Building Block?
- How are building blocks used within the ADM cycle?
- What are the characteristics of an architecture pattern?

11.2 What is a Building Block?

(Syllabus Reference: Unit 10, Learning Outcome 1: You should be able to define what a building block is, and explain what makes a good building block.)

A building block is a package of functionality defined to meet business needs across an organization. A building block has published interfaces to access functionality. A building block may interoperate with other, possibly inter-dependent building blocks.

A good building block has the following characteristics:

- It considers implementation and usage, and evolves to exploit technology and standards
- It may be assembled from other building blocks
- It may be a subassembly of other building blocks
- Ideally, a building block is re-usable and replaceable, and well specified with stable interfaces
- Its specification should be loosely coupled to its implementation, so that it can be realized in several ways without impacting the building block specification

The way in which functionality, products, and custom developments are assembled into building blocks varies widely between individual architectures. Every organization must decide for itself what arrangement of building blocks works best for it. A good choice of building blocks can lead to improvements in legacy system integration, interoperability, and flexibility in the creation of new systems and applications.

An architecture is a composition of:
- A set of building blocks depicted in an architectural model
- A specification of how those building blocks are connected to meet the overall requirements of an information system

The various building blocks in an architecture specify the services required in an enterprise-specific system.

The following general principles should apply:
- An architecture need only contain building blocks to implement those services it requires
- Building blocks may implement one, more than one, or only part of a service identified in the architecture
- Building blocks should conform to standards

11.3 Architecture Building Blocks and Solution Building Blocks

(Syllabus Reference: Unit 10, Learning Outcome 2: You should be able to explain the distinction between Architecture Building Blocks and Solution Building Blocks.)

Systems are built from collections of buildings blocks. They can be defined at many levels of detail:
- Groupings at a functional level, such as a customer database, are known as Architecture Building Blocks
- Real products or specific custom developments are known as Solution Building Blocks

11.3.1 Architecture Building Blocks

Architecture Building Blocks (ABBs) are architecture documentation and models from the enterprise's Architecture Repository classified according to the Architecture Continuum. They are defined or selected during application of the ADM – mainly in Phases A, B, C, and D.

The characteristics of ABBs are as follows:
- They define what functionality will be implemented
- They capture architecture requirements; e.g., Business, Data, Application, and Technology requirements
- They direct and guide the development of Solution Building Blocks

ABB specifications should contain as a minimum:
- Fundamental functionality and attributes: semantic, unambiguous, including security capability and manageability
- Interfaces: chosen set, supplied
- Interoperability and relationship to other building blocks
- Dependent building blocks with required functionality and named user interfaces
- Map to business/organizational entities and policies

Each ABB should include a statement of any architecture documentation and models from the enterprise's Architecture Repository that can be re-used in the architecture development. The specification of building blocks using the ADM is an evolutionary and iterative process.

11.3.2 Solution Building Blocks

Solution Building Blocks (SBBs) relate to the Solutions Continuum. They are implementations of the architectures identified in the enterprise's Architecture Continuum and may be either procured or developed. SBBs appear in Phase E of the ADM where product-specific building blocks are considered for the first time. SBBs define what products and components will implement the functionality, thereby defining the implementation.

The characteristics of SBBs are as follows:
- They define what products and components will implement the functionality
- They define the implementation

- They fulfill business requirements
- They are product or vendor-aware

SBB specifications should contain as a minimum:
- Specific functionality and attributes
- Interfaces: the implemented set
- Required SBBs used with required functionality and names of interfaces used
- Mapping from the SBBs to the IT topology and operational policies
- Specifications of attributes shared such as security, manageability, scalability
- Performance, configurability
- Design drivers and constraints including physical architecture
- Relationships between the SBBs and ABBs

11.4 Building Blocks and the ADM

(Syllabus Reference: Unit 10, Learning Outcome 3: You should be able to briefly explain the use of building blocks in the ADM cycle.)

Systems are built up from collections of building blocks, so most building blocks have to interoperate with other building blocks. Wherever that is true, it is important that the interfaces to a building block are published and reasonably stable.

Building blocks can be defined at various levels of detail, depending on what stage of architecture development has been reached.

For instance, at an early stage, a building block can simply consist of a grouping of functionality, such as a customer database and some retrieval tools. Building blocks at this functional level of definition are described in the TOGAF standard as Architecture Building Blocks (ABBs). Later on, real products or custom developments replace these simple definitions of functionality, and the building blocks are then described as Solution Building Blocks (SBBs).

The key phases and steps of the ADM at which building blocks are evolved and specified are summarized as follows, and illustrated in Figure 26.

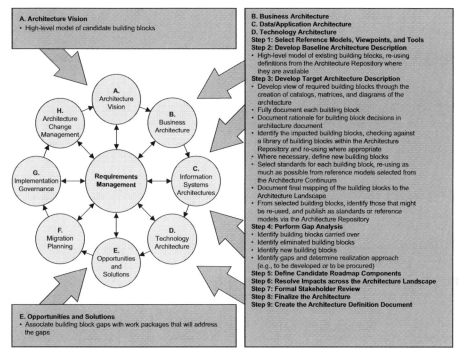

Figure 26: Architecture Building Blocks and their Use in the ADM Cycle

In Phase A, the earliest building block definitions start as relatively abstract entities within the Architecture Vision.

In Phases B, C, and D building blocks within the Business, Data, Application, and Technology Architectures are evolved to a common pattern of steps.

Finally, in Phase E the building blocks become more implementation-specific as SBBs are identified to address gaps.

11.5 Architecture Patterns

(Syllabus Reference: Unit 10, Learning Outcome 4: You should be able to describe the characteristics of an architecture pattern.)

Pattern

A pattern is "an idea that has been useful in one practical context and will probably be useful in others".

[Source: Analysis Patterns – Re-usable Object Models]

In the TOGAF standard, patterns are considered to be a way of putting building blocks into context; for example, to describe a re-usable solution to a problem. Building blocks are what you use; patterns can tell you how you use them, when, why, and what trade-offs you have to make in doing that.

Patterns offer the promise of helping the architect to identify combinations of Architecture and/or Solution Building Blocks (ABBs/SBBs) that have been proven to deliver effective solutions in the past, and may provide the basis for effective solutions in the future.

11.6 Summary

A building block has the following characteristics:
- It is a package of functionality defined to meet the business needs across an organization
- It has published interfaces to access functionality
- It may interoperate with other, inter-dependent building blocks

A good building block:
- Considers implementation and usage and evolves to exploit technology
- May be assembled from other building blocks
- Is re-usable

11.7 Test Yourself Questions

Q1:   Which of the following statements does *not* apply to a building block?
    A.   It is a package of functionality that meets business needs.
    B.   It has published interfaces to access functionality.
    C.   It may interoperate with other building blocks.
    D.   It has a specification that is tightly coupled to its implementation.

Q2:   Which of the following applies to an Architecture Building Block?
    A.   It defines the functionality to be implemented.
    B.   It defines the implementation.
    C.   It defines what products and components will implement the functionality.
    D.   It is product or vendor-aware.

Q3:   Which of the following ADM phases is where SBBs first appear in the
      ADM cycle?
      A.   Phase A
      B.   Phase B
      C.   Phase D
      D.   Phase E
      E.   Phase G

11.8 Recommended Reading

The following are recommended sources of further information for this
chapter:

- The TOGAF Standard, Version 9.2 Part IV: Architecture Content
  Framework, Building Blocks

Chapter 12

ADM Deliverables

12.1 Key Learning Points

This chapter will help you understand the key deliverables of the ADM cycle and their purpose.

Key Points Explained

This chapter will help you to answer the following questions:

- What is the role of architecture deliverables across the ADM cycle?
- What is the purpose of key deliverables?

12.2 The Role of Architecture Deliverables

(Syllabus Reference: Unit 11, Learning Outcome 1: You should be able to briefly explain the role of architecture deliverables across the ADM cycle.)

The TOGAF standard defines a set of suggested deliverables that will be consumed and produced across the TOGAF ADM cycle. The deliverable set provided is intended to provide a typical baseline of architecture deliverables in order to better define the activities required in the ADM and act as a starting point for tailoring within a specific organization.

The TOGAF standard identifies deliverables that are produced as outputs from executing the ADM cycle and potentially consumed as inputs at other points in the ADM. Other deliverables may be produced elsewhere and consumed by the ADM.

As deliverables are typically the contractual or formal work products of an architecture project, it is likely that these deliverables will be constrained or altered by any overarching project or process management for the enterprise (such as CMMI, PRINCE2, PMBOK, or MSP).

[Source: The TOGAF Standard, Version 9.2 Part IV: Architecture Content Framework]

12.3 The Purpose of Key Deliverables

(Syllabus Reference: Unit 11, Learning Outcome 2: For each of the deliverables in this section, you should be able to briefly explain the purpose of the deliverable.)

This section describes the purpose of deliverables consumed and produced across the TOGAF ADM cycle.

12.3.1 Architecture Building Blocks (ABBs)

ABBs are architecture documentation and models from the enterprise's Architecture Repository.

See Chapter 11.

12.3.2 Architecture Contract

Architecture Contracts are the joint agreements between development partners and sponsors on the deliverables, quality, and fitness-for-purpose of an architecture. They are produced in Phase G: Implementation Governance. Successful implementation of these agreements will be delivered through effective Architecture Governance.

By implementing a governed approach to the management of contracts, the following will be ensured:

- A system of continuous monitoring to check integrity, changes, decision-making, and audit of all architecture-related activities within the organization
- Adherence to the principles, standards, and requirements of the existing or developing architectures
- Identification of risks in all aspects of the development and implementation of the architecture(s) covering the internal development against accepted standards, policies, technologies, and products as well as the operational aspects of the architectures such that the organization can continue its business within a resilient environment
- A set of processes and practices that ensure accountability, responsibility, and discipline with regard to the development and usage of all architectural artifacts
- A formal understanding of the governance organization responsible for the contract, their level of authority, and scope of the architecture under the governance of this body

12.3.3 Architecture Definition Document

The Architecture Definition Document is the deliverable container for the core architectural artifacts created during a project and for important related information. The Architecture Definition Document spans all architecture domains (Business, Data, Application, and Technology) and also examines all relevant states of the architecture (baseline, transition, and target).

It is first created in Phase A, where it is populated with artifacts created to support the Architecture Vision. It is updated in Phase B, with Business Architecture-related material, and subsequently updated with Information Systems Architecture material in Phase C, and then with Technology Architecture material in Phase D. Where the scope of change to implement the Target Architecture requires an incremental approach, the Architecture Definition Document will be updated to include one or more Transition Architectures in Phase E.

A Transition Architecture shows the enterprise at an architecturally significant state between the Baseline and Target Architectures. Transition Architectures are used to describe transitional Target Architectures necessary for effective realization of the Target Architecture.

Architecture Definition Document *versus* Architecture Requirements Specification
The Architecture Definition Document is a companion to the Architecture Requirements Specification, with a complementary objective:
The Architecture Definition Document provides a qualitative view of the solution and aims to communicate the intent of the architects.
The Architecture Requirements Specification provides a quantitative view of the solution, stating measurable criteria that must be met during the implementation of the architecture.

12.3.4 Architecture Principles

This set of documentation is an initial output of the Preliminary Phase. Principles are general rules and guidelines, intended to be enduring and seldom amended, that inform and support the way in which an organization sets about fulfilling its mission.

In their turn, principles may be just one element in a structured set of ideas that collectively define and guide the organization, from values through actions to results.

See Section 8.3.

12.3.5 Architecture Repository

The Architecture Repository acts as a holding area for all architecture-related projects within the enterprise. The repository allows projects to manage their deliverables, locate re-usable assets, and publish outputs to stakeholders and other interested parties.

See Sections 3.5 and 6.8.

12.3.6 Architecture Requirements Specification

The Architecture Requirements Specification provides a set of quantitative statements that outline what an implementation project must do in order to comply with the architecture. An Architecture Requirements Specification will typically form a major component of an implementation contract or a contract for more detailed Architecture Definition.

12.3.7 Architecture Roadmap

The Architecture Roadmap lists individual work packages that will realize the Target Architecture and lays them out on a timeline to show progression from the Baseline Architecture to the Target Architecture. The Architecture Roadmap highlights individual work packages' business value at each stage. Transition Architectures necessary to effectively realize the Target Architecture are identified as intermediate steps. The Architecture Roadmap is incrementally developed throughout Phases E and F, and informed by the roadmap components developed in Phases B, C, and D.

12.3.8 Architecture Vision

The Architecture Vision is created in Phase A and provides a high-level summary of the changes to the enterprise that will follow from successful deployment of the Target Architecture. The purpose of the vision is to agree at the outset what the desired outcome should be for the architecture, so that architects can then focus on the detail necessary to validate feasibility. Providing an Architecture Vision also supports stakeholder communication by providing a summary version of the full Architecture Definition.

Business scenarios (see Section 8.5) are a recommended technique that can be used as part of developing an Architecture Vision document.

12.3.9   Business Principles, Business Goals, and Business Drivers

Business principles, business goals, and business drivers provide context for architecture work, by describing the needs and ways of working employed by the enterprise. These will have usually been defined elsewhere in the enterprise prior to the architecture activity. Many factors that lie outside the consideration of architecture discipline may have significant implications for the way that architecture is developed.

2.3.10   Capability Assessment

Before embarking upon a detailed Architecture Definition, it is valuable to understand the baseline and target capability level of the enterprise. This assessment is first carried out in Phase A and updated in Phase E.

This Capability Assessment can be examined on several levels:

- What is the capability level of the enterprise as a whole? Where does the enterprise wish to increase or optimize capability? What are the architectural focus areas that will support the desired development of the enterprise?
- What is the capability or maturity level of the IT function within the enterprise? What are the likely implications of conducting the architecture project in terms of design governance, operational governance, skills, and organization structure? What is an appropriate style, level of formality, and amount of detail for the architecture project to fit with the culture and capability of the IT organization?
- What is the capability and maturity of the architecture function within the enterprise? What architectural assets are currently in existence? Are they maintained and accurate? What standards and reference models need to be considered? Are there likely to be opportunities to create re-usable assets during the architecture project?
- Where capability gaps exist, to what extent is the business ready to transform in order to reach the target capability? What are the risks to transformation, cultural barriers, and other considerations to be addressed beyond the basic capability gap?

12.3.11 Change Request

Requests for Architecture Change are considered in Phase H.

During implementation of an architecture, as more facts become known, it
is possible that the original Architecture Definition and requirements are not
suitable or are not sufficient to complete the implementation of a solution.
In these circumstances, it is necessary for implementation projects to either
deviate from the suggested architectural approach or to request scope
extensions. Additionally, external factors – such as market factors, changes
in business strategy, and new technology opportunities – may open up
opportunities to extend and refine the architecture.

In these circumstances, a Change Request may be submitted in order to
request a dispensation or to kick-start a further cycle of architecture work.

12.3.12 Communications Plan

Enterprise Architectures contain large volumes of complex and inter-
dependent information. Effective communication of targeted information to
the right stakeholders at the right time is a Critical Success Factor (CSF) for
Enterprise Architecture. Development of a Communications Plan in Phase A
for the architecture allows for this communication to be carried out within a
planned and managed process.

12.3.13 Compliance Assessment

Once an architecture has been defined, it is necessary to govern that
architecture through implementation to ensure that the original Architecture
Vision is appropriately realized and that any implementation learnings
are fed back into the architecture process. Periodic compliance reviews of
implementation projects in Phase G provide a mechanism to review project
progress and ensure that the design and implementation is proceeding in-line
with the strategic and architectural objectives.

See Section 9.7.

12.3.14 Implementation and Migration Plan

The Implementation and Migration Plan provides a schedule of the projects
for implementation of Target Architecture. The Implementation and
Migration Plan includes executable projects grouped into managed portfolios

and programs. The Implementation and Migration Strategy identifying the approach to change is a key element of the Implementation and Migration Plan.

> **Development of the Implementation and Migration Plan**
> The outline Implementation and Migration Plan is created in Phase E and then finalized in Phase F.

2.3.15　Implementation Governance Model

Once an architecture has been defined, it is necessary to plan how the Transition Architecture that implements the architecture will be governed through implementation. Within organizations that have established architecture functions, there is likely to be a governance framework already in place, but specific processes, organizations, roles, responsibilities, and measures may need to be defined on a project-by-project basis.

The Implementation Governance Model produced as an output of Phase F ensures that a project transitioning into implementation moves smoothly into appropriate Architecture Governance.

2.3.16　Organizational Model for Enterprise Architecture

An important deliverable of the Preliminary Phase is the Organizational Model for Enterprise Architecture.

In order for an architecture framework to be used successfully, it must be supported by the correct organization, roles, and responsibilities within the enterprise. Of particular importance is the definition of boundaries between different Enterprise Architecture practitioners and the governance relationships that span across these boundaries.

2.3.17　Request for Architecture Work

This is a document that is sent from the sponsoring organization to the architecture organization to trigger the start of an Architecture Development Cycle. Requests for Architecture Work can be created as an output of the

Preliminary Phase, a result of approved architecture Change Requests, or terms of reference for architecture work originating from migration planning.

In general, all the information in this document should be at a high level.

12.3.18 Requirements Impact Assessment

Throughout the ADM, new information is collected relating to an architecture. As this information is gathered, new facts may come to light that invalidate existing aspects of the architecture. A Requirements Impact Assessment assesses the current architecture requirements and specification to identify changes that should be made and the implications of those changes.

12.3.19 Solution Building Blocks

Implementation-specific building blocks from the enterprise's Architecture Repository.

See Chapter 11.

12.3.20 Statement of Architecture Work

The Statement of Architecture Work is created as a deliverable from Phase A and defines the scope and approach that will be used to complete an Architecture Development Cycle. The Statement of Architecture Work is typically the document against which successful execution of the architecture project will be measured and may form the basis for a contractual agreement between the supplier and consumer of architecture services.

12.3.21 Tailored Architecture Framework

Selecting and tailoring a framework is the practical starting point for an architecture project.

The TOGAF standard provides an industry standard framework for architecture that may be used in a wide variety of organizations. However, before the TOGAF framework can be effectively used within an architecture project, tailoring at two levels is necessary.

Firstly, it is necessary to tailor the TOGAF model for integration into the enterprise. This tailoring will include integration with management frameworks, customization of terminology, development of presentational styles, selection, configuration, and deployment of architecture tools, etc. The formality and detail of any frameworks adopted should also align with other contextual factors for the enterprise, such as culture, stakeholders, commercial models for Enterprise Architecture, and the existing level of Architecture Capability.

Once the framework has been tailored to the enterprise, further tailoring is necessary in order to fit the framework to the specific architecture project. Tailoring at this level will select appropriate deliverables and artifacts to meet project and stakeholder needs.

12.4 Summary

Architecture deliverables are the contractual or formal work products of an architecture project. The descriptions provided by the TOGAF standard are a baseline and thus a starting point for tailoring.

12.5 Test Yourself Questions

Q1: Which of the following best describes the role of architecture deliverables?
  A. They are defined so as to avoid tailoring the TOGAF framework.
  B. They are defined as a starting point for tailoring the TOGAF framework.
  C. They are used to measure the progress made in architecture development.
  D. They are used to report to the stakeholders.

Q2: Which of the following acts as a holding area for all architecture-related projects within the enterprise?
  A. Architecture Building Block
  B. Architecture Repository
  C. Architecture Roadmap
  D. Architecture Vision

Q3:   Which of the following documents acts as the deliverable container for the Business, Data, Application, and Technology architectural artifacts?
A.   Architecture Contract
B.   Architecture Definition Document
C.   Architecture Requirements Specification
D.   Architecture Roadmap
E.   Architecture Vision

Q4:   Which of the following documents is produced early in the project lifecycle and contains a summary view of the end architecture project?
A.   Architecture Contract
B.   Architecture Definition Document
C.   Architecture Requirements Specification
D.   Architecture Roadmap
E.   Architecture Vision

Q5:   Which of the following documents is produced in Phase A as a response to the Request for Architecture Work?
A.   Architecture Contract
B.   Architecture Definition Document
C.   Requirements Impact Statement
D.   Statement of Architecture Work

12.6 Recommended Reading

The following are recommended sources of further information for this chapter:

- The TOGAF Standard, Version 9.2 Part IV: Architecture Content Framework, Architecture Deliverables

Chapter 13

TOGAF Reference Models

13.1 Key Learning Points

This chapter will help you understand two example TOGAF Reference Models provided in the TOGAF Library.

Key Points Explained

This chapter will help you to answer the following questions:

- What is the TOGAF Technical Reference Model (TRM)?
- What are the main components of the TOGAF TRM?
- What are the basic concepts of the Integrated Information Infrastructure Reference Model (III-RM)?
- What is the relationship of the III-RM to the concept of Boundaryless Information Flow?

13.2 The TOGAF TRM as a Foundation Architecture

(Syllabus Reference: Unit 12, Learning Outcome 1: You should be able to explain the role of the TRM as a Foundation Architecture.)

A Foundation Architecture is an architecture of building blocks and corresponding standards that supports all the Common Systems Architectures, and, therefore, the complete computing environment. A Foundation Architecture is positioned at the left-hand side of the Enterprise Continuum.

The TOGAF Library includes the Technical Reference Model (TRM) as an example Foundation Architecture. The TOGAF TRM describes a fundamental architecture upon which other, more specific, architectures can be based.

> **Platform-centric**
>
> This TRM is "platform-centric": it focuses on the services and structure of the
> underlying platform necessary to support the use and re-use of applications
> (i.e., application portability). In particular, it centers on the interfaces between
> that platform and the supported applications, and between the platform and the
> external environment.

Major characteristics of a Foundation Architecture include the following:

- It reflects general computing requirements
- It reflects general building blocks
- It defines technology standards for implementing these building blocks
- It provides direction for products and services
- It reflects the function of a complete, robust computing environment that can be used as a foundation
- It provides open system standards, directions, and recommendations
- It reflects directions and strategies

(Syllabus Reference: Unit 12, Learning Outcome 2: You should be able to describe at a high level the main components of the TRM.)

The TRM has two main components:

1. A taxonomy that defines terminology, and provides a coherent description of the components and conceptual structure of an information system
2. A model, with an associated TRM graphic, that provides a visual representation of the taxonomy, as an aid to understanding

Figure 27 shows the high-level model of the TRM. The three main parts of the TRM (Application Software, Application Platform, and Communications Infrastructure) are connected by two interfaces (Application Platform Interface and Communications Infrastructure Interface).

Figure 27:   Technical Reference Model – High-Level Model View

Figure 28 shows the detail of the TRM. This highlights the platform service categories (these are covered in detail in the TOGAF 9 Level 2 syllabus) together with the external environment entities, such as applications and Communications Infrastructure.

Figure 28:   Detailed Technical Reference Model (Showing Service Categories)

13.3 The Integrated Information Infrastructure Reference Model

(Syllabus Reference: Unit 12, Learning Outcome 3: You should be able to briefly explain the basic concepts of the III-RM.)

With the emergence of Internet-based technologies, many organizations shifted their main focus of attention, and the main return on investment in architecture effort, from the "platform-centric" Application Platform space, modeled by the TRM, to the Application Software space. In response to this, The Open Group developed the Integrated Information Infrastructure Reference Model (III-RM).

The III-RM is a reference model that focuses on the Application Software space, and is a "Common Systems Architecture" in Enterprise Continuum terms. The III-RM is a subset of the TOGAF TRM in terms of its overall scope, but it also expands certain parts of the TRM – in particular, the business applications and infrastructure applications parts – in order to provide help in addressing one of the key challenges facing the Enterprise Architect today: the need to design an integrated information infrastructure to enable Boundaryless Information Flow. These concepts are explained in detail below.

Like the TOGAF TRM, the III-RM has two main components:
1. A taxonomy, which defines terminology, and provides a coherent description of the components and conceptual structure of an integrated information infrastructure
2. An associated III-RM graphic, which provides a visual representation of the taxonomy, and the inter-relationship of the components, as an aid to understanding

Figure 29:   III-RM High-Level View

It is fundamentally an Application Architecture reference model – a model of the application components and application services software essential for an integrated information infrastructure. It includes information provider and consumer applications, as well as brokering applications. Further detail is covered in the TOGAF 9 Certified Syllabus.

III-RM

The Open Group has documented the business scenario that led to the creation of the Integrated Information Infrastructure Reference Model (III-RM) in the Interoperable Enterprise Business Scenario (Doc. No. K022). This is freely available for download from the Business Scenarios section of The Open Group Library at www.opengroup.org/library.

13.4 Boundaryless Information Flow

(Syllabus Reference: Unit 12, Learning Outcome 4: You should be able to briefly explain the relationship of the III-RM to the concept of Boundaryless Information Flow.)

The Boundaryless Information Flow problem space is one that is shared by many customer members of The Open Group, and by many similar organizations worldwide. It is essentially the problem of getting information to the right people at the right time in a secure, reliable manner, in order to support the operations that are core to the extended enterprise.

In General Electric, Jack Welch invented the term "the Boundaryless Organization", not to imply that there are no boundaries, but that they should be made permeable.

Creating organizational structures that enabled each individual department to operate at maximum efficiency was for a long time accepted as the best approach to managing a large enterprise. Among other benefits, this approach fostered the development of specialist skills in staff, who could apply those skills to specific aspects of an overall activity (such as a manufacturing process), in order to accomplish the tasks involved better, faster, and cheaper.

As each overall activity progressed through the organization, passing from department to department (for example, from Design to Production to Sales), each department would take inputs from the previous department in the process, apply its own business processes to the activity, and send its output to the next department in line.

In today's world where speed, flexibility, and responsiveness to changing markets make the difference between success and failure, this method of working is not appropriate. Organizations have been trying for some time to overcome the limitations imposed by traditional organization structures. Many business process re-engineering efforts have been undertaken and abandoned because they were too ambitious, while others cost far more in both time and money than originally intended.

However, organizations recognize that they need not abandon functional or departmental organization altogether. They can enable the right people to come together in cross-functional teams so that all the skills, knowledge, and expertise can be brought to bear on any specific problem or business opportunity.

But this in turn poses its own challenges. CIOs are under enormous pressure to provide access to information to each cross-functional team on an as-required basis, and yet the sources of this data can be numerous and the volumes huge.

Even worse, the IT systems, which have been built over a period of 20 or 30 years at a cost of many billions of dollars, and are not about to be thrown out or replaced wholesale, were built for each functional department. So although it may be possible to get people to work together effectively (no minor achievement in itself), the IT systems they use are designed to support the old-style thinking. The IT systems in place today do not allow for information to flow in support of the boundaryless organization. When they do, then we will have Boundaryless Information Flow.

The Open Group Interoperable Enterprise Business Scenario crystallizes this need for Boundaryless Information Flow and describes the way in which this need drives IT customers' deployment of their information infrastructure.

In this scenario, the customer's problem statement says that the customer enterprise could gain significant operational efficiencies and improve the many different business processes of the enterprise – both internal processes, and those spanning the key interactions with suppliers, customers, and partners – if only it could provide staff with:

- **Integrated information** so that different and potentially conflicting pieces of information are not distributed throughout different systems
- **Integrated access to that information** so that staff can access all the information they need and have a right to, through one convenient interface

The infrastructure that enables this vision is termed the "integrated information infrastructure".

One of the key challenges for the architect in today's enterprise is to work out, and then communicate to senior management, how far technologies such as web services, application integration services, etc. can go toward achieving an integrated information infrastructure, and realizing the vision of Boundaryless Information Flow, in the enterprise concerned.

Follow-up analysis by The Open Group of the Interoperable Enterprise
Business Scenario resulted in the development of an integrated information
infrastructure model (the III-RM), which depicts the major components
required to address the Boundaryless Information Flow problem space, and
can help the architect in this task.

The III-RM thus provides insights related to customer needs for
Boundaryless Information Flow in enterprise environments. The model also
points to rules and standards to assist in leveraging solutions and products
within the value chain.

Boundaryless Information Flow

A shorthand representation of "access to integrated information to support
business process improvements" representing a desired state of an enterprise's
infrastructure specific to the business needs of the organization.
[Source: The TOGAF Standard, Version 9.2 Part I: Introduction, Definitions]
The need for Boundaryless Information Flow – a trademark of The Open Group –
is described in the TOGAF® Series Guide: The TOGAF Integrated Information
Infrastructure Reference Model (III-RM).

13.5 Summary

The TOGAF Technical Reference Model provides a model and core
taxonomy of generic platform services. In summary:

- It is "platform-centric"
- It is a Foundation Architecture
- It can be used to build any system architecture
- A taxonomy defines consistent terminology

The III-RM is a model of the key components for developing, managing, and
operating an integrated information infrastructure. In summary:

- It is an example of a Common Systems Architecture
- The focus is on applications rather than the platform
- It has two main components: a taxonomy and an associated graphic

- A key driver for development of the model is the need for Boundaryless Information Flow; getting information to the right people at the right time in a secure, reliable, and timely manner

13.6 **Test Yourself Questions**

Q1:   Which of the following is *not* a characteristic of the TOGAF
      Foundation Architecture?
      A.   It reflects general building blocks.
      B.   It defines open standards for building blocks implementation.
      C.   It provides open systems standards.
      D.   It provides guidelines for testing collections of systems.
      E.   It reflects general computing requirements.

Q2:   Which of the following best describes the purpose of the TRM?
      A.   To provide a framework for IT governance
      B.   To provide a visual model, terminology, and coherent description
           of components and structure of an information system
      C.   To provide a method for architecture development
      D.   To provide a system engineering viewpoint on a possible solution

Q3:   Where is the TOGAF Technical Reference Model positioned in terms
      of the Enterprise Continuum?
      A.   The left-hand side of the Architecture Continuum
      B.   The right-hand side of the Architecture Continuum
      C.   The left-hand side of the Solutions Continuum
      D.   The right-hand side of the Solutions Continuum

Q4:   Which of the following architecture domains does the III-RM
      describe?
      A.   Business
      B.   Data
      C.   Application
      D.   Technology

Q5: How is the III-RM classified in terms of the Enterprise Continuum?
   A. Industry Solution
   B. Foundation Architecture
   C. Common Systems Architecture
   D. Common Systems Solution

Q6: Which of the following was a key driver for the development of the III-RM?
   A. Boundaryless Information Flow
   B. Clinger-Cohen
   C. PRINCE2
   D. Sarbanes-Oxley

13.7 Recommended Reading

The following are recommended sources of further information for this chapter:

- TOGAF® Series Guide: The TOGAF Integrated Information Infrastructure Reference Model (III-RM)
- TOGAF® Series Guide: The TOGAF Technical Reference Model (TRM)

Appendix A

Answers to Test Yourself Questions

A.1 Answers to the Test Yourself Questions

This appendix contains a table of the answers to the Test Yourself Questions organized by chapter of the Study Guide.

Reference	Answer	Notes
Chapter 1	Q1. B	The TOGAF 9 Part 1 Examination has 40 simple multiple-choice questions. It is closed book. The policy requires one month before a retake. The exam coverage includes two building block questions.
	Q2. B	TOGAF 9 Foundation is the entry-level qualification. Options C and D do not exist as options within the program.
	Q3. C	These match the principles stated in the Certification Policy document.
	Q4. D	Guidelines for adapting the ADM: Iteration and Levels is part of the Level 2 Syllabus for the TOGAF 9 Certified qualification. It is not part of the TOGAF 9 Foundation Syllabus.
Chapter 2	Q1. B	The TOGAF standard is both an architecture framework and a method for architecture development.
	Q2. E	All of the reasons given are reasons for needing an architecture framework.
	Q3. C	The TRM is an example Foundation Architecture, which is contained in a TOGAF Series Guide within the TOGAF Library.
	Q4. E	Pattern Architecture is not one of the four, which are BDAT: Business, Data, Application, and Technology Architecture.
	Q5. B	Part II: the ADM.

Reference	Answer	Notes
Chapter 6	Q1. A	It is a virtual repository of all assets produced during application of the ADM.
	Q2. A	Deliverables from previous architecture work.
	Q3. D	All of the answers apply.
	Q4. C	The two continua are the constituent parts.
	Q5. A	The III-RM is a Common Systems Architecture.
	Q6. D	ABBs are part of the Architecture Continuum.
	Q7. A	Systems libraries
	Q8. A	The Architecture Repository
	Q9. D	Reference Library
	Q10. A	Capability Architectures
	Q11. B	Standards compliance is used as part of Architecture Governance.
Chapter 7	Q1. C	Phase C: Information Systems Architectures
	Q2. A	The Preliminary Phase
	Q3. B	Develop a high-level aspirational vision of the capabilities and business value to be delivered as a result of the proposed Enterprise Architecture.
	Q4. A	Creation of the Architecture Vision occurs in Phase A.
	Q5. C	Capability Maturity models are recommended.
	Q6. B	Phase A commences with receipt of the Request for Architecture Work.
	Q7. A	Business Scenarios
	Q8. B	Business Architecture is undertaken first so as to demonstrate the business value of subsequent architecture work to key stakeholders.
	Q9. B	Business rules, job descriptions are considered relevant in Phase B.
	Q10. C	The III-RM
	Q11. A	Phase E generates the outline Implementation and Migration Strategy.
	Q12. B	Phase F
	Q13. C	Phase G

Reference	Answer	Notes
	Q14. D	Ensure the Architecture Governance Framework is executed.
	Q15. D	Simplification change
	Q16. A	Architecture Requirements are managed across all phases of the ADM.
Chapter 8	Q1. D	Requirements Management handles the flow of requirements.
	Q2. C	Rationale
	Q3. B	Specific
	Q4. B	Phase A when creating the Architecture Vision.
	Q5. B	If correctly eliminated you would not add it back to the target.
	Q6. C	Presentation Interoperability
	Q7. D	It is for determining the readiness of an organization to accept change.
	Q8. B	It is the residual risk after mitigating actions have been taken.
	Q9. C	It is a business planning technique focussed on business outcomes.
Chapter 9	Q1. B	It is the Architecture Board that manages the activity.
	Q2. A	Expenditure control is not included.
	Q3. C	All actions and their decision support will be available for inspection.
	Q4. A	Compliance is part of process.
	Q5. D	Budgetary control is outside.
	Q6. E	These are all benefits.
	Q7. A	Resourcing
	Q8. B	The agreement is between development partners and sponsors.
	Q9. C	Where no features are in common then it is termed Irrelevant.
	Q10. A	Architecture Board
	Q11. D	Phase D: Technology Architecture

Reference	Answer	Notes
Chapter 10	Q1. D	Stakeholder
	Q2. A	It is the other way round; an architecture viewpoint is considered a template for an architecture view.
	Q3. D	They are not synonymous as concerns are used to derive requirements.
	Q4. B	A and C should be one *or more* stakeholders/concerns; D is incorrect.
Chapter 11	Q1. D	Building blocks should have a loose coupling to implementation to allow for multiple implementations and re-implementation.
	Q2. A	ABBs define functionality – not implementation.
	Q3. D	Phase E
Chapter 12	Q1. B	The TOGAF framework should be tailored for use.
	Q2. B	The Architecture Repository
	Q3. B	The Architecture Definition Document
	Q4. E	Architecture Vision
	Q5. D	The Statement of Architecture Work
Chapter 13	Q1. D	Testing guidelines are not included.
	Q2. B	It is a visual model and taxonomy.
	Q3. A	It is at the left-hand side, the most generic, of the Architecture Continuum.
	Q4. C	It is an Application Architecture reference model.
	Q5. C	It is a Common Systems Architecture.
	Q6. A	The Boundaryless Information Flow problem space led to development of the III-RM.

Test Yourself Examination Papers

B.1 Examination Papers

The purpose of this appendix is to provide two examination papers that will allow you to assess your knowledge of the TOGAF 9 Foundation Syllabus.

Prior to attempting these examination papers you should have worked through this Study Guide section by section, answering the Test Yourself questions and reading the referenced sections from the TOGAF document. If you have completed your preparation, then you can then attempt these examination papers. If not, please spend some time preparing as suggested.

The examination papers provided in this appendix use a simple multiple-choice format, which is the same as the certification examination. Each question has one single correct answer, that scores one point.

Please read each question carefully before reading the answer options. Be aware that some questions may seem to have more than one right answer, but you are to look for the one that makes the most sense and is the most correct. See Appendix C for the answers.

B.2 Test Yourself Examination Paper 1

Item 1

Question:

Which one of the following best describes the TOGAF standard?

A. A framework and method for architecture development

B. An architecture pattern

C. A method for developing Technology Architectures

D. A method for IT Governance

Item 2

Question:

Which part of the TOGAF standard provides a number of architecture development phases?

A. Introduction
B. Architecture Development Method (ADM)
C. ADM Guidelines and Techniques
D. Architecture Content Framework
E. Enterprise Continuum and Tools

Item 3

Question:

According to the TOGAF standard, all of the following are suggested characteristics of an architecture framework, *except* _____

A. A common vocabulary
B. A list of recommended standards
C. A method for designing a target state of the enterprise in terms of building blocks
D. A set of structures which can be used to develop a broad range of architectures
E. A software development lifecycle method

Item 4

Question:

Which of the TOGAF Architecture Development phases includes the development of Data and Application Architectures?

A. Phase A
B. Phase B
C. Phase C
D. Phase D
E. Phase E

Item 5

Question:

Which one of the following does the Architecture Content Framework describe as a work product that is contractually specified, formally reviewed, and signed off by the stakeholders?

A. An artifact
B. A building block
C. A catalog
D. A deliverable
E. A matrix

Item 6

Question:

Which of the following best completes the sentence: The Enterprise Continuum _____

A. describes a database of open industry standards
B. is an architecture framework
C. is a technical reference model
D. provides a method for architecture development
E. provides methods for classifying artifacts

Item 7

Question:

According to the TOGAF standard, in which ADM phase does the initial implementation planning occur?

A. Phase A: Architecture Vision
B. Phase B: Business Architecture
C. Phase C: Information Systems Architectures
D. Phase D: Technology Architecture
E. Phase E: Opportunities and Solutions

Item 8

Question:

According to the TOGAF standard, which of the following is the reason why the first execution of an ADM cycle will be more difficult than later cycles?

A. Because there are few architecture assets available

B. Because of lack of governance

C. Because of insufficient trained architecture practitioners

D. Because the Baseline Architecture must be fully defined across the enterprise

Item 9

Question:

As architecture deliverables and work products created in one ADM phase are modified by subsequent phases, how does the TOGAF standard suggest tracking the changes?

A. Change control committee

B. Document checkpoints and journaling

C. Version numbers

D. Workflow management system

Item 10

Question:

Complete the sentence: The architectures that address the detailed enterprise needs and business requirements within the Architecture Continuum are known as_____

A. Foundation Architectures

B. Industry Architectures

C. Common Systems Architectures

D. Organization-Specific Architectures

Item 11

Question:

According to the TOGAF standard, which one of the following is described as a view of the Architecture Repository and provides methods for classifying architecture and solution artifacts as they evolve?

A. Architecture Landscape
B. Architecture Governance Repository
C. Enterprise Continuum
D. Governance Log
E. Standards Information Base

Item 12

Question:

Which one of the following represents the detailed construction of the architectures defined in the Architecture Continuum?

A. Architecture Building Blocks
B. Foundation Architectures
C. Reference Models
D. Solution Building Blocks

Item 13

Question:

An organization has bought a large enterprise application. As a result, which of the following could be included in the organization's Solutions Continuum?

A. A reference implementation of the Foundation Architecture
B. A reference implementation of the Technical Reference Model for the organization
C. Architecture Building Blocks for the organizations' Industry-Specific Architecture
D. Product information for purchased products

Item 14

Question:

Complete the sentence: All of the following are technology-related drivers for architecture Change Requests, *except* _____

A. asset management cost reductions

B. new technology reports

C. standards initiatives

D. strategic change

E. technology withdrawal

Item 15

Question:

Complete the sentence: In Phase C, when an existing application is to be replaced, the Data Architecture should_____

A. be re-factored to align with the technology infrastructure

B. describe how this change impacts other projects

C. identify the data migration requirements

D. include the application interoperability requirements

E. estimate the effort required to overcome any issues

Item 16

Question:

The approach of the Preliminary Phase is about defining "where, what, why, who, and how we do architecture" in the enterprise concerned.   Which one of the following statements is *not* correct?

A. "Where" can be seen as scoping the enterprise concerned

B. "Why" can be seen as the key drivers and elements in the context of the organization

C. "Who" can be seen as defining the sponsor responsible for performing the architectural work

D. "How" is determined by the frameworks selected and the methodologies that are going to be used

Item 17

Question:

In which phase of the ADM are the gap analysis results from the four architecture domains taken into account?

A. Phase E
B. Phase F
C. Phase G
D. Phase H
E. Requirements Management

Item 18

Question:

In Phase D, which of the following resources from the Architecture Repository should be considered in the development of the Technology Architecture?

A. Architecture Vision
B. Business rules, job descriptions
C. Implementation and Migration Plan
D. Stakeholder Map
E. TOGAF Technical Reference Model

Item 19

Question:

Complete the sentence: All of the following are part of the approach to the Preliminary Phase, *except* _____

A. defining the enterprise
B. identifying key drivers and elements in the organizational context
C. defining Architecture Contracts
D. defining the framework to be used
E. defining the requirements for architecture work

Item 20

Question:

In which phase of the TOGAF ADM do activities include assessing the dependencies, costs, and benefits of the migration projects?

A. Phase E

B. Phase F

C. Phase G

D. Phase H

E. Requirements Management

Item 21

Question:

Complete the sentence: Phase A is initiated upon receipt of _____

A. approval from the Chief Information Officer

B. a directive from the Chief Executive Officer

C. a Request for Architecture Work from the sponsoring organization

D. the Requirements Analysis document

Item 22

Question:

Complete the sentence: Business Architecture is the first architecture activity undertaken since _____

A. it focuses on identifying and defining the key applications used in the enterprise

B. it provides knowledge that is a prerequisite for undertaking work in the other architecture domains

C. it defines the physical realization of an architectural solution

D. it finalizes the Architecture Vision and Architecture Definition Documents

E. it mobilizes supporting operations to support the ongoing architecture development

Item 23

Question:

Complete the sentence: According to the TOGAF standard, Capability-Based Planning is _____

A. a tactical planning technique that enhances system performance
B. focused on technical capabilities
C. focused on staffing and human resource management issues
D. focused on business outcomes

Item 24

Question:

In which phase of the ADM is an initial assessment of Business Transformation Readiness performed?

A. Preliminary Phase
B. Phase A
C. Phase B
D. Phase E
E. Phase F

Item 25

Question:

Which of the following is defined as the risk categorization after the implementation of mitigating actions?

A. Actual Level of Risk
B. Initial Level of Risk
C. Residual Level of Risk
D. Strategic Level of Risk

Item 26

Question:

Which one of the statements about Architecture Principles is *not* correct?

A. A good set of principles is complete.
B. A principle is a general rule or guideline.
C. A principle is transient and updated frequently.
D. A principle statement should be succinct and unambiguous.
E. They are described in a standard way.

Item 27

Question:

What technique does the TOGAF standard recommend for identifying and understanding the requirements that an architecture must address?

A. Stakeholder management
B. Risk management
C. Gap analysis
D. Business scenarios
E. Architecture Principles

Item 28

Question:

Gap analysis is a key step in validating the architecture in Phase B: Business ArchitecturE. Which one of the following statements is true?

A. Gap analysis highlights services that are available
B. Gap analysis highlights the impacts of change
C. Gap analysis highlights services that are yet to be procured
D. Gap analysis identifies areas where the Data Architecture needs to change
E. Gap analysis can be used to resolve conflicts amongst different viewpoints

Item 29

Question:

According to the TOGAF standard, which of the following best describes why an Architecture Board should be established?

A. To conduct source code design reviews
B. To ensure that new systems are introduced in a managed change process
C. To facilitate the adoption of advanced technologies
D. To oversee the implementation of the governance strategy

Item 30

Question:

The TOGAF standard defines levels of architecture conformance.

Which of the following describes a situation where some features in an architecture specification have not been implemented, but those that have are in accordance with the specification?

A. Compliant

B. Conformant

C. Consistent

D. Irrelevant

E. Non-conformant

Item 31

Question:

Which Architecture Governance process ensures that regulatory requirements are being met?

A. Business control

B. Compliance

C. Dispensation

D. Environment management

E. Policy management

Item 32

Question:

When applying a cycle of the ADM with the Architecture Vision to establish an Architecture Capability, which phase does TOGAF Part VII recommend defines the structure of the organization's Architecture Repository?

A. Application Architecture

B. Business Architecture

C. Data Architecture

D. Preliminary Phase

E. Technology Architecture

Item 33

Question:

Architecture views and architecture viewpoints are used by an architect to capture or model the design of a system architecture. Which one of the following statements is true?

A. An architecture view is the perspective of an individual stakeholder.
B. An architecture viewpoint is the perspective of an individual stakeholder.
C. Different stakeholders always share the same architecture views.
D. Different stakeholders always share the same architecture viewpoints.

Item 34

Question:

Stakeholders and their concerns are key concepts in the TOGAF standard. Which one of the following statements is false?

A. Concerns are interests relevant to one or more stakeholders.
B. Stakeholders can be individuals, teams, or organizations.
C. Stakeholders have key roles in, or concerns about, the system.
D. Concerns should be SMART and have specific metrics.

Item 35

Question:

Which of the following is considered by the TOGAF standard as an attribute of a good building block?

A. A building block that is re-usable
B. A building block meeting business needs
C. A building block with public interfaces
D. A building block that guides the development of solutions
E. A building block that is product-aware

Item 36

Question:

Which one of the following best describes the content of an Architecture Building Block?

A. Defined implementation
B. Fundamental functionality
C. Products and components used to implement the functionality
D. Product or vendor-aware
E. Specific functionality

Item 37

Question:

Which one of the following statements does *not* correctly describe architecture deliverables?

A. They are consumed and produced across the ADM cycle
B. They are defined to avoid tailoring the inputs and outputs of the ADM cycle
C. They are typically contractual work products of an architecture project
D. They are usually reviewed and signed off by the stakeholders

Item 38

Question:

What TOGAF deliverable identifies changes that are needed to the current architecture requirements and specification, and also documents the implications of change?

A. Requirements Impact Assessment
B. Architecture Vision
C. Gap Analysis Results
D. Architecture Landscape
E. Architecture Roadmap

Item 39

Question:

Which of the following best describes the purpose of the TOGAF TRM?

A. To provide a generic framework for IT governance
B. To provide a list of standards
C. To provide a method for architecture development
D. To provide a system engineering viewpoint on a possible solution
E. To provide a visual model, and core terminology for generic platform services

Item 40

Question:

Where does the Integrated Information Infrastructure Reference Model fit in terms of the Enterprise Continuum?

A. Common Systems Architectures
B. Foundation Architectures
C. Industry Architectures
D. Organization-Specific Architectures

B.3 Test Yourself Examination Paper 2

Item 41

Question:

Which section of the TOGAF standard describes the processes, skills, and roles to establish and operate an architecture function within an enterprise?

A. Part II: Architecture Development Method
B. Part III: ADM Guidelines and Techniques
C. Part IV: Architecture Content Framework
D. Part VI: Architecture Capability Framework

Item 42

Question:

Complete the sentence: To promote effective architectural activity within the enterprise, the TOGAF standard recommends the establishment of a(n)

_____

A. Enterprise Architecture Capability
B. IT Governing Board
C. Program Management Office
D. Quality Assurance department
E. Service Management department

Item 43

Question:

Which phase of the ADM is used to finalize a set of Transition Architectures that will support implementation?

A. Phase D
B. Phase E
C. Phase F
D. Phase G
E. Phase H

Item 44

Question:

Which one of the following statements best describes the ADM Guidelines and Techniques?

A. Guidelines address different usage scenarios including different process styles and specialist architectures that can be adapted in the ADM.

B. Guidelines address different usage scenarios that cannot be adapted directly into the ADM iteration process.

C. Techniques support different usage scenarios that can be adapted directly into the ADM iteration process.

D. Techniques support different usage scenarios including different process styles and specialist architectures that can be adapted in the ADM.

Item 45

Question:

According to the TOGAF standard, the recommended dimensions used to define the scope of an architecture include all the following, *except:*

A. Architecture Domains

B. Breadth

C. Depth

D. Subject Matter

E. Time Period

Item 46

Question:

Which of the following classes of architectural information within the Architecture Repository defines processes that support governance of the Architecture Repository?

A. Architecture Capability

B. Architecture Landscape

C. Architecture Metamodel

D. Governance Log

E. Reference Library

Item 47

Question:

In which ADM phase are the business principles, business goals, and strategic drivers validated?

A. Preliminary Phase
B. Phase A: Architecture Vision
C. Phase B: Business Architecture
D. Phase H: Architecture Change Management
E. Requirements Management Phase

Item 48

Question:

Which section of the TOGAF standard describes the purpose of deliverables produced as outputs from the ADM cycle?

A. ADM Guidelines and Techniques
B. Architecture Capability Framework
C. Architecture Content Framework
D. Architecture Governance Framework
E. TOGAF Reference Models

Item 49

Question:

Which of the following best describes the TOGAF Technical Reference Model?

A. The TOGAF Architecture Development Method mandates the use of the Technical Reference Model for large complex architecture projects.
B. The Technical Reference Model is an integral part of the TOGAF Architecture Development Method.
C. The Technical Reference Model should not be modified.
D. The Technical Reference Model includes a set of graphical models and a corresponding taxonomy.

Item 50

Question:

Which one of the following best describes a primary use of the Architecture Vision document?

A. A checklist for compliance reviews

B. To calculate detailed cost estimates

C. To project plan the implementation activities

D. To describe the benefits of the proposed capability to stakeholders

Item 51

Question:

Which of the following could be considered for potential use in Phase C: Application Architecture?

A. The ARTS data model

B. The Integrated Information Infrastructure Reference Model

C. The Resource-Event-Agent model

D. The STEP framework

E. The TOGAF Technical Reference Model

Item 52

Question:

In Phase G, what document establishes the connection between the architecture organization and the implementation organization?

A. Architecture Contract

B. Architecture Landscape

C. Architecture Roadmap

D. Requirements Impact Statement

E. Transition Architecture

Item 53

Question:

Which phase of the ADM is an ongoing activity that is visited throughout a TOGAF architecture project?

A. Architecture Change Management

B. Implementation Governance

C. Migration Planning

D. Preliminary Phase

E. Requirements Management

Item 54

Question:

Which of the following statements is true about risk management in the ADM?

A. Risk analysis is best conducted in the Architecture Vision phase so that the risk is eliminated in subsequent phases.
B. Risk analysis should be carried out first in the Migration Planning phase.
C. Risk is pervasive in all Enterprise Architecture activity and should be managed in all phases of the ADM.
D. The only risks that are within the scope of Enterprise Architecture are technological risks.

Item 55

Question:

Which of the following best describes Capability-Based Planning?

A. A business planning technique that focuses on business outcomes
B. A business planning technique that focuses on horizontal capabilities
C. A business planning technique that focuses on vertical capabilities
D. A human resource planning technique that focuses on capable architect

Item 56

Question:

According to the TOGAF standard, which one of the following is the practice by which the Enterprise Architecture and other architectures are managed and controlled at an enterprise level?

A. Architecture Governance
B. Corporate governance
C. IT governance
D. Technology governance

Item 57

Question:

Which one of the following is recommended to achieve a customer-focused, value-adding, and sustainable architecture practice?

A. Develop an Architecture Roadmap
B. Populate the Architecture Repository
C. Populate the Enterprise Continuum
D. Use the Architecture Development Method
E. Use the Implementation Governance Phase

Item 58

Question:

Which of the following statements best describes the purpose of the Architecture Requirements Specification?

A. A document that triggers the start of an Architecture Development Cycle
B. A qualitative view of the solution to communicate the intent of the architect
C. A quantitative view of the solution to measure the implementation
D. A record of deviations from the planned architectural approach to identify changes to be made

Item 59

Question:

Which one of the following best describes the purpose of the Communications Plan?

A. To ensure that architecture information is communicated to the right stakeholders at the right time
B. To support Boundaryless Information Flow
C. To evangelize the architecture to the end-user community
D. To keep the Architecture Review Board appraised of changes to the architecture
E. To ensure that the outcomes of a Compliance Assessment are distributed to the members of the Architecture Review Board

Item 60

Question:

Complete the sentence: The statement "Getting information to the right people at the right time in a secure, reliable manner in order to support the operations that are core to the extended enterprise" describes the concept of

_____

A. Boundaryless Information Flow
B. Interoperability
C. Portability
D. Service-Oriented Architecture

Item 61

Question:

According to the TOGAF standard, where should Architecture Governance artifacts be stored?

A. In the Architecture Repository
B. In the Foundation Architecture
C. In the Integrated Infrastructure Reference Model
D. In the Requirements Repository
E. In the Standards Information Base

Item 62

Question:

Which architecture domain describes logical software and hardware capabilities?

A. Application Architecture
B. Business Architecture
C. Data Architecture
D. Information Systems Architecture
E. Technology Architecture

Item 63

Question:

Which of the following lists components within the Architecture Repository?

A. Organizational Metamodel, Architecture Capability, Architecture Landscape, Best Practices, Reference Library, Compliance Strategy
B. Architecture Metamodel, Organizational Capability Model, Application Landscape, SIB, Reference Library, Governance Model
C. Business Metamodel, Architecture Capability, Architecture Landscape, SIB, Reference Library, Governance Log
D. Architecture Metamodel, Architecture Capability, Architecture Landscape, SIB, Reference Library, Governance Log

Item 64

Question:

Which of the following reasons best describes why the ADM numbering scheme for versioning output is an example and not mandatory?

A. To show the evolution of deliverables
B. To permit adaptation as required
C. To enable use with the Architecture Content Framework
D. To support change management

Item 65

Question:

Which of the following is *not* one of the domain architectures produced by the TOGAF ADM process?

A. Application Architecture
B. Business Architecture
C. Data Architecture
D. Pattern Architecture
E. Technology Architecture

Item 66

Question:

Which of the TOGAF ADM phases is considered to be the initial phase of an Architecture Development Cycle?

A. Preliminary Phase
B. Phase A
C. Phase B
D. Phase E
E. Phase G

Item 67

Question:

Which one of the following is defined as describing the state of an architecture at an architecturally significant point in time during the progression from the Baseline to the Target Architecture?

A. Capability Architecture
B. Foundation Architecture
C. Segment Architecture
D. Solution Architecture
E. Transition Architecture

Item 68

Question:

Which one of the following best describes ADM Phase F?

A. Prepare the organization for successful architecture projects
B. Develop architectures in four domains
C. Perform initial implementation planning
D. Develop detailed implementation plan
E. Provide architecture oversight for the implementation

Item 69

Question:

Complete the sentence: The TOGAF Integrated Information Infrastructure Reference Model
(III-RM) is classified in the Architecture Continuum as an example of a(n)

_____

A. Common Systems Architecture
B. Industry Architecture
C. Enterprise Architecture
D. Foundation Architecture

Item 70

Question:

Which of the ADM phases includes the objective of establishing the organizational model for Enterprise Architecture?

A. Preliminary
B. Phase A
C. Phase B
D. Phase D
E. Phase E

Item 71

Question:

Which of the following is a technique that can be used to discover and document business requirements in Phase A?

A. Business Scenarios
B. Business Transformation Readiness Assessment
C. Capability-Based Planning
D. Gap Analysis
E. Stakeholder Management

Item 72

Question:

Complete the sentence: The Transition Architectures defined in Phase E are confirmed with the stakeholders in _____

A. Phase E

B. Phase F

C. Phase G

D. Phase H

Item 73

Question:

Complete the sentence: A good business scenario should be "SMART". The letter "S" stands for _____

A. Solution-oriented

B. Specific

C. Strategic

D. Stakeholder-oriented

Item 74

Question:

Which of the following best describes the Business Transformation Readiness Assessment technique?

A. A technique to define the degree to which information and services are to be shared

B. A technique used to validate an architecture

C. A technique used to identify and understand the business requirements an architecture must address

D. A technique used to develop general rules and guidelines for the architecture being developed

E. A technique used to understand the readiness of an organization to accept change

Item 75

Question:

Which of the following best describes the Capability-Based Planning technique?

A. A technique used to plan the degree to which information and services are to be shared
B. A technique used to validate an architecture
C. A technique used for business planning that focuses on business outcomes
D. A technique used to develop general rules and guidelines for the architecture being developed

Item 76

Question:

Which one of the following best describes an Architecture Contract?

A. An agreement between the development partners and stakeholders on the acceptable risks and mitigating actions for an architecture
B. An agreement between development partners and sponsors on the deliverables, quality, and fitness-for-purpose of an architecture
C. An agreement between the lead architect and the development partners on the enforcement of Architecture Compliance for an architecture
D. An agreement between development partners and sponsors on how best to monitor implementation of the architecture

Item 77

Question:

The TOGAF standard defines a set of terms to describe Architecture Compliance.   Which one of the following applies to the case where an implementation has no features in common with the architecture specification?

A. Compliant
B. Conformant
C. Irrelevant
D. Non-conformant

Item 78

Question:

Which of the following terms does the TOGAF standard use to describe people who have an interest in a system?

A. Architect
B. Consumer
C. Sponsor
D. Stakeholder

Item 79

Question:

Which of the following ADM phases is where SBBs first appear in the ADM cycle?

A. Phase A
B. Phase B
C. Phase D
D. Phase E
E. Phase G

Item 80

Question:

Which of the following documents acts as the deliverable container for the Business, Data, Application, and Technology architectural artifacts?

A. Architecture Contract
B. Architecture Definition Document
C. Architecture Requirements Specification
D. Architecture Roadmap
E. Architecture Vision

Test Yourself Examination Paper Answers

This appendix contains the answers to the Examination Papers in Appendix B.

C.1 Scoring the Examinations

For each question, award yourself one point for each correct answer.

The target score for each examination is 28 points or more out of 40 (70%). Note that at the time of writing the certification examination has a pass mark lower than this test yourself examination, so if you can make the target you should be ready to take the real examination.

C.2 Answers to Test Yourself Examination Paper 1

Item 1   A
This is the best answer. The TOGAF standard is a framework – a detailed method and a set of supporting tools – for developing an Enterprise Architecture.

Item 2   B
Part II: Architecture Development Method describes the TOGAF Architecture Development Method (ADM) – a step-by-step approach to developing an Enterprise Architecture in a number of phases.

Item 3   E
An architecture framework is a foundational structure, or set of structures, which can be used for developing a broad range of different architectures. It should describe a method for designing a target state of the enterprise in terms of a set of building blocks, and for showing how the building blocks fit together. It should contain a set of tools and provide a common vocabulary. It should also include a list of recommended standards and compliant products that can be used to implement the building blocks.

Item 4   C

Phase C: Information Systems Architectures describes the development of Information Systems Architectures for an architecture project, including the development of Data and Application Architectures.

Item 5   D

A deliverable is a work product that is contractually specified and in turn formally reviewed, agreed, and signed off by the stakeholders. Deliverables represent the output of projects and those deliverables that are in documentation form will typically be archived at completion of a project, or transitioned into an Architecture Repository as a reference model, standard, or snapshot of the Architecture Landscape at a point in time.

Item 6   E

The Enterprise Continuum is a model providing methods for classifying architecture and solution artifacts as they evolve from generic Foundation Architectures to Organization-Specific Architectures. The Enterprise Continuum comprises two complementary concepts: the Architecture Continuum and the Solutions Continuum.

Item 7   E

Phase E: Opportunities & Solutions conducts initial implementation planning and the identification of delivery vehicles for the architecture defined in the previous phases.

Item 8   A

The first execution of the ADM will often be the hardest, since the architecture assets available for re-use will be relatively scarce. Even at this stage of development, however, there will be architecture assets available from external sources such as the TOGAF Library, as well as the IT industry at large, that could be leveraged in support of the effort.

Item 9   C

Output is generated throughout the ADM process, and output in an early phase may be modified in a later phase. The TOGAF standard recommends that the versioning of output is managed through version numbers. In all cases, the ADM numbering scheme is provided as an example. It should be adapted by the architect to meet the requirements of the organization and to work with the architecture tools and repositories employed by the organization.

Item 10 D
Organization-Specific Architectures are viewed as being at the right end of the Architecture Continuum, and are the most relevant to the IT customer community, since they describe and guide the final deployment of solution components for a particular enterprise or extended network of connected enterprises.

Item 11 C
The Enterprise Continuum provides a view of the Architecture Repository that shows the evolution of these related architectures from generic to specific, from abstract to concrete, and from logical to physical.

Item 12 D
The Solutions Continuum defines what is available in the organizational environment as re-usable Solution Building Blocks (SBBs).

Item 13 D
The Solutions Continuum is a population of the architecture with reference building blocks – either purchased products or built components – that represent a solution to the enterprise's business need expressed at that level.

Item 14 D
Strategic change is a business driver.

Item 15 C
When an existing application is replaced, there will be a critical need to migrate data (master, transactional, and reference) to the new application. The Data Architecture should identify data migration requirements and also provide indicators as to the level of transformation, weeding, and cleansing that will be required to present data in a format that meets the requirements and constraints of the target application.

Item 16 C
"Who" is to identify the sponsor stakeholder(s) and other major stakeholders impacted by the business directive to create an Enterprise Architecture

and determine their requirements and priorities from the enterprise, their
relationships with the enterprise, and required working behaviors with each
other. Note in this answer it incorrectly suggests that the sponsor performs
the work.

Item 17   A
In Phase E the gap analysis results from all architecture domains are taken
into account.

Item 18   E
The TOGAF TRM should be considered in the development of the
Technology Architecture in Phase D.

Item 19   C
Architecture Contracts are prepared and issued in Phase G.

Item 20   B
Phase F activities include assessing the dependencies, costs, and benefits of
the various migration projects.

Item 21   C
Phase A starts with receipt of a Request for Architecture Work from the
sponsoring organization to the architecture organization.

Item 22   B
A knowledge of the Business Architecture is a prerequisite for architecture
work in any other domain (Data, Application, Technology), and is therefore
the first architecture activity that needs to be undertaken, if not catered for
already in other organizational processes (enterprise planning, strategic
business planning, business process re-engineering, etc.).

Item 23   D
Capability-Based Planning is a business planning technique that focuses on
business outcomes. It focuses on the planning, engineering, and delivery
of strategic business capabilities to the enterprise. It is business-driven and
business-led and combines the requisite efforts of all lines of business to
achieve the desired capability. Capability-Based Planning accommodates
most, if not all, of the corporate business models and is especially useful

in organizations where a latent capability to respond (e.g., an emergency preparedness unit) is required and the same resources are involved in multiple capabilities.

Item 24   B
Business Transformation Readiness is first assessed in Phase A, so actions can be worked into Phases E and F in the Implementation and Migration Plan.

Item 25   C
The risk categorization after implementation of mitigating actions is known as "Residual Level of Risk".

Item 26   C
Principles are intended to be enduring and seldom amended.

Item 27   D
Business scenarios are an important technique that may be used at various stages of the Enterprise Architecture, principally the Architecture Vision and the Business Architecture, but in other architecture domains as well, if required, to derive the characteristics of the architecture directly from the high-level requirements of the business. They are used to help identify and understand business needs, and thereby to derive the business requirements that the architecture development has to address.

Item 28   C
A key step in validating an architecture is to consider what may have been forgotten.

Item 29   D
A key element in a successful Architecture Governance strategy is a cross-organization Architecture Board to oversee the implementation of the strategy.

Item 30   A
The TOGAF standard describes "compliant" as a situation where some features in an architecture specification have not been implemented, but those that have are in accordance with the specification.

Item 31   B

The Compliance process ensures regulatory requirements are being met.

Item 32   C

The Data Architecture phase would define the structure of the organization's Enterprise Continuum and Architecture Repository.

Item 33   B

A view is what you see. A viewpoint is where you are looking from – the vantage point or perspective that determines what you see.

Item 34   D

"Concerns" are the interests in a system relevant to one or more of its stakeholders, and determine the acceptability of the system. Concerns may pertain to any aspect of the system's functioning, development, or operation, including considerations such as performance, reliability, security, distribution, and evolvability. The terms "concern" and "requirement" are not synonymous. Concerns are the root of the process of decomposition into requirements. Concerns are represented in the architecture by these requirements. Requirements should be SMART (e.g., specific metrics).

Item 35   A

The TOGAF standard considers re-usability an attribute of a good building block.

Item 36   B

An ABB has fundamental functionality and attributes: semantic, unambiguous, including security capability and manageability.

Item 37   B

The TOGAF standard provides a typical baseline of architecture deliverables in order to better define the activities required in the ADM and act as a starting point for tailoring within a specific organization.

Item 38   A

Throughout the ADM, new information is collected relating to an architecture. As this information is gathered, new facts may come to light that invalidate existing aspects of the architecture. A Requirements

Impact Assessment assesses the current architecture requirements and specification to identify changes that should be made and the implications of those changes.

Item 39   E

The TOGAF Foundation Architecture is an architecture of generic services and functions that provides a foundation on which more specific architectures and architectural components can be built. This Foundation Architecture is embodied within the Technical Reference Model (TRM), which provides a model and taxonomy of generic platform services.

Item 40   A

The TOGAF Integrated Information Infrastructure Reference Model (III-RM) is a Common Systems Architecture that focuses on the requirements, building blocks, and standards relating to the vision of Boundaryless Information Flow.

C.3 Answers to Test Yourself Examination Paper 2

Item 41   E

The Architecture Capability Framework discusses the organization, processes, skills, roles, and responsibilities required to establish and operate an architecture practice within an enterprise.

Item 42   A

An Enterprise Architecture Capability (or Architecture Capability), in the context of the TOGAF standard, is the ability for an organization to effectively undertake the activities of an Enterprise Architecture practice.

Item 43   C

Phase F confirms the Transition Architectures defined in Phase E with the relevant stakeholders and finalizes them.

Item 44   A

Part III contains a collection of guidelines and techniques for use in applying the TOGAF standard and the ADM. The guidelines document how to adapt the ADM process and specialist architecture styles, whereas the techniques are used when applying the ADM process.

Item 45   D
The recommended dimensions to define the scope of an architecture activity are breadth, depth, time period, and architecture domains.

Item 46   A
The Architecture Capability defines the parameters, structures, and processes that support governance of the Architecture Repository.

Item 47   B
Phase A: Architecture Vision includes the validation of business principles, goals, strategic drivers, and also Key Performance Indicators (KPIs).

Item 48   C
The Architecture Content Framework provides a detailed model of architectural work products, including deliverables and their purpose, artifacts within deliverables, and the Architecture Building Blocks (ABBs) that deliverables represent.

Item 49   D
The TOGAF TRM has two main components: 1. A taxonomy that defines terminology, and provides a coherent description of the components and conceptual structure of an information system. 2. A model, with an associated TRM graphic, that provides a visual representation of the taxonomy, as an aid to understanding.

Item 50   D
The Architecture Vision provides the sponsor with a key tool to sell the benefits of the proposed capability to stakeholders and decision-makers within the enterprise. It describes how the new capability will meet the business goals and strategic objectives and address the stakeholder concerns when implemented.

Item 51   B
The TOGAF Library includes the Reference Model for Integrated Information Infrastructure (III-RM) that could be considered for use in this

phase. It focuses on the application-level components and services necessary to provide an integrated information infrastructure.

Item 52   A
Architecture Contracts are the joint agreements between development partners and sponsors on the deliverables, quality, and fitness-for-purpose of an architecture. They are produced in Phase G.

Item 53   E
The process of managing architecture requirements applies to all phases of the ADM cycle. As shown by its central placement in the ADM cycle diagram, this process is central to driving the ADM process.

Item 54   C
Risk is pervasive in any Enterprise Architecture activity and present in all phases within the ADM.

Item 55   A
Capability-Based Planning is a business planning technique that focuses on business outcomes. It is business-driven and business-led and combines the requisite efforts of all lines of business to achieve the desired capability. It accommodates most, if not all, of the corporate business models and is especially useful in organizations where a latent capability to respond (e.g., an emergency preparedness unit) is required and the same resources are involved in multiple capabilities.

Item 56   A
Architecture Governance is the practice by which Enterprise Architectures and other architectures are managed and controlled at an enterprise-wide level.

Item 57   D
The Architecture Capability Framework recommends applying the ADM with the specific Architecture Vision to establish a sustainable architecture practice within an organization.

Item 58   C
The Architecture Requirements Specification provides a set of quantitative statements that outline what an implementation project must do in order to comply with the architecture.

Item 59   A
Effective communication of targeted information to the right stakeholders at the right time is a Critical Success Factor (CSF) for Enterprise Architecture. Development of a Communications Plan in Phase A for the architecture allows for this communication to be carried out within a planned and managed process.

Item 60   A
Boundaryless Information Flow is essentially the problem of getting information to the right people at the right time in a secure, reliable manner, in order to support the operations that are core to the extended enterprise.

Item 61   A
Architecture Governance artifacts should be stored in the Architecture Repository.

Item 62   E
The Technology Architecture includes the software and hardware capabilities that are required to support the deployment of business, data, and application services. This includes IT infrastructure, middleware, networks, communications, processing, and standards.

Item 63   D
Components of the Architecture Repository are the Architecture Metamodel, Architecture Capability, Architecture Landscape, SIB, Reference Library, and Governance Log. In addition, in the TOGAF Standard, Version 9.2, are the Architecture Requirements Repository and the Solutions Landscape.

Item 64   B
The numbering scheme provided in the TOGAF ADM for its outputs is intended as an example. It should be adapted by the architect to meet the requirements of the organization and to work with the architecture tools and repositories employed by the organization.

Item 65   D

Pattern Architecture is not one of the four domain architectures, which are BDAT: Business, Data, Application, and Technology Architecture.

Item 66   B

Phase A: Architecture Vision is the initial phase of a cycle. Note that the Preliminary Phase is a preparatory phase. Phase A: Architecture Vision describes the initial phase of an Architecture Development Cycle. It includes information about defining the scope, identifying the stakeholders, creating the Architecture Vision, and obtaining approvals.

Item 67   E

A Transition Architecture is defined as a formal description of one state of the architecture at an architecturally significant point in time. One or more Transition Architectures may be used to describe the progression in time from the Baseline to the Target Architecture.

Item 68   D

Phase F: Migration Planning develops the detailed Implementation and Migration Plan that addresses how to move from the Baseline to the Target Architecture.

Item 69   A

The III-RM is a Common Systems Architecture. The TOGAF Integrated Information Infrastructure Reference Model (III-RM) is a reference model that supports describing Common Systems Architecture in the Application domain that focuses on the requirements, building blocks, and standards relating to the vision of Boundaryless Information Flow.

Item 70   A

The Preliminary Phase has as part of its objectives establishment of the Architecture Capability; it includes defining and establishing the Organizational Model for Enterprise Architecture.

Item 71   A

Business scenarios are an appropriate and useful technique to discover and document business requirements in Phase A, and to articulate an Architecture Vision that responds to those requirements.

Item 72   B

The Transition Architectures are confirmed in Phase F. An objective of Phase F is to ensure that the business value and cost of work packages and Transition Architectures is understood by key stakeholders.

Item 73   B

The S in SMART stands for Specific. SMART is defined as follows: **Specific**, by defining what needs to be done. **Measurable**, through clear metrics for success. **Actionable**, by clearly segmenting the problem and providing the basis for a solution. **Realistic**, in that the problem can be solved within the bounds of physical reality, time, and cost constraints. **Time-bound**, in that there is a clear statement of when the opportunity expires.

Item 74   E

The Business Transformation Readiness Assessment technique is used for determining the readiness of an organization to accept change. Enterprise Architecture often involves considerable change. It provides a technique for understanding the readiness of an organization to accept change, identifying the issues, and dealing with them in the Implementation and Migration Plan. It is based on the Canadian Government Business Transformation Enablement Program (BTEP).

Item 75   C

Capability-Based Planning is a business planning technique that focuses on business outcomes. It is business-driven and business-led and combines the requisite efforts of all lines of business to achieve the desired capability. It accommodates most, if not all, of the corporate business models and is especially useful in organizations where a latent capability to respond (e.g., an emergency preparedness unit) is required and the same resources are involved in multiple capabilities. Often the need for these capabilities is discovered and refined using business scenarios.

Item 76   B

The agreement is between development partners and sponsors. Architecture Contracts are joint agreements between development partners and sponsors on the deliverables, quality, and fitness-for-purpose of an architecture. Successful implementation of these agreements will be delivered through effective Architecture Governance. Taking a governed approach to contract management ensures a system that continuously monitors integrity, changes, decision-making, and audit, as well as adherence to the principles, standards, and requirements of the enterprise. The architecture team may also be included in product procurement, to help minimize the opportunity for misinterpretation of the Enterprise Architecture.

Item 77   C
Where no features are in common then it is termed Irrelevant.

Item 78   D
Stakeholders are people who have interests in a system; for example, users, developers, etc. Stakeholders can be individuals, teams, organizations, etc. A system has one or more stakeholders. Each stakeholder typically has interests in, or concerns relative to, that system.

Item 79   D
SBBs appear in Phase E of the ADM where product-specific building blocks are considered for the first time. SBBs define what products and components will implement the functionality, thereby defining the implementation.

Item 80   B
The Architecture Definition Document is the deliverable container for the core architectural artifacts created during a project and for important related information. The Architecture Definition Document spans all architecture domains (Business, Data, Application, and Technology) and also examines all relevant states of the architecture (Baseline, Transition, and Target).

Appendix D

TOGAF 9 Foundation Syllabus

This appendix provides a copy of the Level 1 Learning Units that comprise the syllabus for the TOGAF 9 Foundation certification. Each learning outcome is phrased in terms of what the candidate should have learned. The KLP[13] references can be used to trace the requirement back to sections of the TOGAF standard.

D.1 Basic Concepts

UNIT 1	Basic Concepts
Purpose	The purpose of this Learning Unit is to introduce the basic concepts of Enterprise Architecture and the TOGAF framework.
KLP Reference	1-*, 2-*
Learning Outcome	The Candidate must be able to: 1. Describe what an enterprise is (KLP 1.3-1) 2. Explain the purpose of an Enterprise Architecture (KLP 1.3-2) 3. List the business benefits of having an Enterprise Architecture (KLP 1.3-3) 4. Define what an Architecture Framework is (KLP 1.3-4) 5. Explain why the TOGAF standard is suitable as a framework for Enterprise Architecture (KLP 1.3-5) 6. Describe the structure of the TOGAF standard, and briefly explain the contents of each of the parts (KLP 1.1-1, 1.1-2) 7. Briefly explain what the TOGAF standard is (KLP 2.1-1) 8. Explain what architecture is in the context of the TOGAF standard (KLP 2.2-1) 9. List the different types of architecture that the TOGAF standard deals with (KLP 2.3-1) 10. Briefly explain the TOGAF Library (KLP 1.2-1)

---

13   KLP is an abbreviation for Key Learning Point. A learning outcome comprises one or more key learning points.

D.2 Core Concepts

UNIT 2	Core Concepts
Purpose	The purpose of this Learning Unit is to help the Candidate explain the core concepts of the TOGAF standard.
KLP Reference	2-*, 29.1-1
Learning Outcome	The Candidate must be able to define and explain the following core concepts: 1. The ADM: phase names and the purpose of each phase (high-level) (KLP 2.4-1) 2. The Architecture Content Framework: deliverables, artifacts, and building blocks (KLP 2.5-1, 29.1-1) 3. The Enterprise Continuum (KLP 2.6-1) 4. The Architecture Repository (KLP 2.7-1) 5. Establishing and maintaining an Enterprise Architecture Capability (KLP 2.8-1) 6. Establishing the Architecture Capability as an operational entity (KLP 2.9-1) 7. How to use the TOGAF standard with other frameworks (KLP 2.10-1)

D.3 General Definitions

UNIT 3	General Definitions
Purpose	The purpose of this Learning Unit is to help the Candidate understand the key terminology of the TOGAF standard.
KLP Reference	3-*
Learning Outcome	The Candidate must be able to understand and explain the following definitions from Chapter 3: 1. Application Architecture (KLP 3.3-1) 2. Architectural Style (KLP 3.6-1) 3. Architecture (KLP 3.7-1) 4. Architecture Building Block (ABB) (KLP 3.8-1) 5. Architecture Continuum (KLP 3.9-1) 6. Architecture Development Method (ADM) (KLP 3.10-1) 7. Architecture Domain (KLP 3.11-1) 8. Architecture Framework (KLP 3.12-1) 9. Architecture Governance (KLP 3.13-1) 10. Architecture Principle (KLP 3.16-1)

UNIT 3	General Definitions
	11. Architecture View (KLP 3.17-1) 12. Architecture Viewpoint (KLP 3.18-1) 13. Architecture Vision (KLP 3.19-1) 14. Artifact (KLP 3.20-1) 15. Baseline (KLP 3.21-1) 16. Building Block (KLP 3.23-1) 17. Business Architecture (KLP 3.24-1) 18. Business Capability (KLP 3.25-1) 19. Business Governance (KLP 3.27-1) 20. Capability (KLP 3.30-1) 21. Concern (KLP 3.34-1) 22. Course of Action (KLP 3.35-1) 23. Data Architecture (KLP 3.36-1) 24. Deliverable (KLP 3.37-1) 25. Enterprise (KLP 3.38-1) 26. Foundation Architecture (KLP 3.40-1) 27. Gap (KLP 3.42-1) 28. Governance (KLP 3.43-1) 29. Information (KLP 3.44-1) 30. Information Technology (IT) (KLP 3.46-1) 31. Logical (KLP 3.48-1) 32. Metadata (KLP 3.49-1) 33. Metamodel (KLP 3.50-1) 34. Method (KLP 3.51-1) 35. Modeling (KLP 3.52-1) 36. Objective (KLP 3.54-1) 37. Physical (KLP 3.57-1) 38. Reference Model (RM) (KLP 3.59-1) 39. Repository (KLP 3.60-1) 40. Requirement (KLP 3.61-1) 41. Service (KLP 3.65-1) 42. Solution Architecture (KLP 3.69-1) 43. Solution Building Block (SBB) (KLP 3.70-1) 44. Stakeholder (KLP 3.72-1) 45. Strategic Architecture (KLP 3.74-1) 46. Target Architecture (KLP 3.75-1) 47. Technology Architecture (KLP 3.77-1) 48. Transition Architecture (KLP 3.80-1) 49. Value Stream (KLP 3.81-1) 50. Viewpoint Library (KLP 3.82-1) Note: It is expected that these definitions would be covered as part of the learning in other units.

D.4 Introduction to the ADM

UNIT 4	Introduction to the ADM
Purpose	The purpose of this Learning Unit is to help the Candidate understand the ADM cycle, briefly explain the objective of each phase in the cycle, and how to adapt and scope the ADM for use.
KLP Reference	2-*, 4-*
Learning Outcome	The Candidate must be able to: 1. Briefly describe the ADM cycle, and its phases (KLP 2.4-1, 4.2.2-1, -2, -3) 2. Describe a typical set of steps, such as those for Phases B, C, and D (KLP 4.2.2-2) 3. Describe the versioning convention for deliverables used in Phases A to D (KLP 4.2.2-3) 4. Briefly describe the relationship between the ADM and the Enterprise Continuum, Architecture Repository, Foundation Architecture, and Supporting Guidelines and Techniques (KLP 4.1-1) 5. Explain the purpose of the supporting guidelines and techniques, and the difference between guidelines and techniques (KLP 4.1-2) 6. Briefly describe the key points of the ADM cycle (KLP 4.2.1-1) 7. List the main reasons why you would need to adapt the ADM (KLP 4.3-1) 8. Explain the need for the ADM process to be governed (KLP 4.4-1) 9. Describe the major information areas managed by a governance repository (KLP 4.4-2) 10. Briefly explain the reasons for scoping an architecture activity (KLP 4.5-1) 11. List the possible dimensions for limiting the scope (KLP 4.5-2) 12. Briefly explain the need for an integration framework that sits above individual architectures (KLP 4.6-1)

D.5 Enterprise Continuum and Tools

UNIT 5	Enterprise Continuum and Tools
Purpose	The purpose of this Learning Unit is to help the Candidate understand the concept of the Enterprise Continuum, its purpose, and constituent parts.
KLP Reference	35-*, 37-*
Learning Outcome	The Candidate must be able to: 1. Briefly explain what the Enterprise Continuum is (KLP 35.1-1) 2. Explain how it is used in organizing and developing an architecture (KLP 35.2-1) 3. Explain how the Enterprise Continuum promotes re-use of architecture artifacts (KLP 35.2-2) 4. Describe the constituents of the Enterprise Continuum (KLP 35.3-1) 5. Explain the purpose of the Enterprise Continuum (KLP 35.3-2) 6. Explain the purpose of the Architecture Continuum (KLP 35.4-3) 7. List the stages of architecture evolution defined in the Architecture Continuum (KLP 35.4-4) 8. Explain the purpose of the Solutions Continuum (KLP 35.4-6) 9. List the stages of architecture evolution defined in the Solutions Continuum (KLP 35.4-7) 10. Explain the relationship between the Enterprise Continuum and the ADM (KLP 35.5-1) 11. Describe the Architecture Repository (KLP 37-1) 12. Explain the relationship between the Enterprise Continuum and the Architecture Repository (KLP 35.1-2, 37.1-2) 13. Describe the classes of information held in the Architecture Repository (KLP 37.1-2) 14. List the three levels of the Architecture Landscape (KLP 37.2-1) 15. Explain the purpose of the Standards Information Base within the Architecture Repository (KLP 37.4-1)

D.6 ADM Phases (Level 1)

UNIT 6	ADM Phases (Level 1)
Purpose	The purpose of this Learning Unit is to help the Candidate understand how each of the ADM phases contributes to the success of Enterprise Architecture by understanding the *objectives*, and the *approach* for each phase.
KLP Reference	5-*, 6-*, 7-*, 8-*, 9-*, 10-*, 11-*, 12-*, 13-*, 14-*, 15-*, 16-*

Learning Outcome	**Preliminary Phase:** The Candidate must be able to:
	1. Describe the main objectives of the phase (KLP 5.1-1)
	2. Briefly explain the seven aspects of the approach undertaken in this phase (KLP 5.5-1):
	    Defining the enterprise
	    Identifying key drivers and elements in the organizational context
	    Defining the requirements for architecture work
	    Defining the Architecture Principles that will inform any architecture work
	    Defining the framework to be used
	    Defining the relationships between management frameworks
	    Evaluating the Enterprise Architecture maturity
	Phase A: The Candidate must be able to:
	1. Describe the main objectives of the phase (KLP 6.1-1)
	2. Briefly explain the main aspect to the approach in this phase (KLP 6.5-1):
	    — Creating the Architecture Vision
	Phase B: The Candidate must be able to:
	1. Describe the main objectives of the phase (KLP 7.1-1)
	2. Briefly explain the main aspects of the approach in this phase (KLP 7.5-1):
	    — General
	    — Developing the Baseline Description
	    — Applying Business Capabilities
	    — Applying Value Streams
	    — Applying the Organization Map
	    — Applying Modeling Techniques
	    — Using the Architecture Repository
	Phase C: The Candidate must be able to:
	1. Describe the main objectives of the phase (KLP 8.1-1, 9.1-1, 10.1-1)
	2. Briefly explain the approach recommended by the TOGAF framework, including:
	    — Key considerations for the Data Architecture (KLP 9.5-1)
	    — Using the Architecture Repository (KLP 9.5-1, 10.5-1)

UNIT 6	ADM Phases (Level 1)
	Phase D: The Candidate must be able to: 1. Describe the main objectives of the phase (KLP 11.1-1) 2. Briefly explain the approach to the phase (KLP 11.5-1), including: — Emerging technologies – a driver for change — Using the Architecture Repository **Phase E**: The Candidate must be able to: 1. Describe the main objectives of the phase (KLP 12.1-1) 2. Briefly explain the approach to the phase (KLP 12.5-1) **Phase F**: The Candidate must be able to: 1. Describe the main objectives of the phase (KLP 13.1-1) 2. Briefly explain the approach to the phase (KLP 13.5-1) **Phase G**: The Candidate must be able to: 1. Describe the main objectives of the phase (KLP 14.1-1) 2. Briefly explain the approach to the phase (KLP 14.5-1) **Phase H**: The Candidate must be able to: 1. Describe the main objectives of the phase (KLP 15.1-1) 2. Briefly explain the approach to the phase (KLP 15.5-1), including: — Drivers for change — Enterprise Architecture management process — Guidelines for maintenance *versus* architecture redesign **ADM Architecture Requirements Management**: The Candidate must be able to: 1. Briefly explain how Requirements Management fits into the ADM cycle (KLP 16.1-1) 2. Describe the nature of the Requirements Management process (KLP 16.1-2) 3. Describe the approach to Requirements Management (KLP 16.5-1)

D.7 ADM Guidelines and Techniques

UNIT 7	ADM Guidelines and Techniques
Purpose	The purpose of this Learning Unit is to introduce the Candidate to the ADM Guidelines and Techniques available to support application of the ADM.
KLP Reference	17-*, 20-*, BS-*, 23-*, 25-*, 26-*, 27-*, 28-*
Learning Outcome	The Candidate must be able to: 1. Briefly explain the contents of Part III, ADM Guidelines and Techniques (KLP 17.1-1) 2. Briefly explain the need for Architecture Principles and where they are used within the TOGAF ADM (KLP 20.1-1) 3. Describe the recommended template for Architecture Principles (KLP 20.3-1) 4. Explain what makes a good Architecture Principle (KLP 20.4-2) 5. Understand what a Business Scenario is and its purpose (KLP BS.1-1) 6. Explain where Business Scenarios are used within the ADM cycle (KLP BS.1-2) 7. Explain the purpose of Gap Analysis (KLP 23.2-1) 8. Describe the Gap Analysis technique (KLP 23.2-1) 9. Explain the term interoperability (KLP 25.2-1) 10. Understand the use of Interoperability Requirements within the TOGAF ADM (KLP 25.1-1) 11. Understand Business Transformation Readiness Assessment (KLP 26.1-2) 12. Understand where Business Transformation Readiness Assessment is used within the ADM (KLP 26.1-1) 13. Understand the characteristics of Risk Management (KLP 27.1-2) 14. Understand where Risk Management is used within the TOGAF ADM (KLP 27.1-1) 15. Understand Capability-Based Planning (KLP 28.1-1) 16. Briefly explain the use of the TOGAF ADM in the context of a specific architectural style (KLP 17.3-1)

D.8 Architecture Governance (Level 1)

UNIT 8	Architecture Governance (Level 1)
Purpose	The purpose of this Learning Unit is to help the Candidate understand how Architecture Governance contributes to the Architecture Development Cycle.
KLP Reference	40-*, 41-*, 42-*, 43-*, 44-*
Learning Outcome	The Candidate must be able to: 1. Briefly explain the concept of Architecture Governance (KLP 44.1-1) 2. Describe the main concepts that make up an Architecture Governance framework (KLP 44.2-1) 3. Explain why Architecture Governance is beneficial (KLP 44.3-1) 4. Briefly explain the need for establishment of an Architecture Board (KLP 41.1-1) 5. List the responsibilities of an Architecture Board (KLP 41.2-1) 6. Briefly explain the role of Architecture Contracts (KLP 43.1-1) 7. Briefly explain the meaning of Architecture Compliance (KLP 42.2-1) 8. Briefly explain the need for Architecture Compliance (KLP 42.1-1) 9. Briefly explain the purpose of Architecture Compliance Reviews (KLP 42.3-1) 10. Briefly describe the Architecture Compliance Review process (KLP 42.4-1) 11. Briefly explain how the ADM can be used to establish an Architecture Capability (KLP 40.1-1)

D.9 Architecture Views, Viewpoints, and Stakeholders

UNIT 9	Architecture Views, Viewpoints, and Stakeholders
Purpose	The purpose of this Learning Unit is to help the Candidate understand the concepts of views and viewpoints, and their role in communicating with stakeholders as well as applying them to the Architecture Development Cycle.
KLP Reference	31-*

Learning Outcome	The Candidate must be able to:
	1. Define and explain the following key concepts (KLP 31.1-1):
	  — Stakeholders
	  — Concerns
	  — Architecture Views
	  — Architecture Viewpoints
	2. Describe a simple example of an architecture viewpoint and view (KLP 31.1-2)
	3. Discuss the relationship between stakeholders, concerns, views, and viewpoints (KLP 31.1-3)
	4. Describe the architecture view creation process (KLP 31.2-1)

D.10 Building Blocks

UNIT 10	Building Blocks
Purpose	The purpose of this Learning Unit is to help the Candidate understand the concept of building blocks within the TOGAF standard.
KLP Reference	22-*, 33-*
Learning Outcome	The Candidate must be able to: 1. Define what a building block is, and explain what makes a good building block (KLP 33.2-1) 2. Explain the distinction between Architecture Building Blocks and Solution Building Blocks (KLP 33.2-2) 3. Briefly explain the use of building blocks in the ADM cycle (KLP 33.3-1) 4. Describe the characteristics of an Architecture Pattern (KLP 22.1-1)

D.11 ADM Deliverables

UNIT 11	ADM Deliverables
Purpose	The purpose of this Learning Unit is to help the Candidate understand key deliverables of the ADM cycle.
KLP Reference	32.1-1, 32.2-1

Learning Outcome	The Candidate must be able to:
	 1. Briefly explain the role of architecture deliverables across the ADM cycle (KLP 32.1-1)
	 2. Briefly explain the purpose of the following deliverables (KLP 32.2-1):
	    — Architecture Building Blocks
	    — Architecture Contract
	    — Architecture Definition Document
	    — Architecture Principles
	    — Architecture Repository
	    — Architecture Requirements Specification
	    — Architecture Roadmap
	    — Architecture Vision
	    — Business Principles, Business Goals, and Business Drivers
	    — Capability Assessment
	    — Change Request
	    — Communications Plan
	    — Compliance Assessment
	    — Implementation and Migration Plan
	    — Implementation Governance Model
	    — Organizational Model for Enterprise Architecture
	    — Request for Architecture Work
	    — Requirements Impact Assessment
	    — Solution Building Blocks
	    — Statement of Architecture Work
	    — Tailored Architecture Framework
	 Note: It is expected that at least some of these deliverables would be covered as part of the learning in other units.

D.12 TOGAF Reference Models (Level 1)

UNIT 12	TOGAF Reference Models (Level 1)
Purpose	The purpose of this Learning Unit is to introduce the two example TOGAF Reference Models documented in the TOGAF Series Guides.
KLP Reference	TRM-*, IIIRM-*
Learning Outcome	The Candidate must be able to: 1. Explain the role of the TRM as a Foundation Architecture (KLP TRM.2-1) 2. Describe at a high level the main components of the TOGAF TRM (KLP TRM.4-1) 3. Briefly explain the basic concepts of the III-RM (KLP IIIRM.1-1) 4. Briefly explain the relationship of the III-RM to the concept of Boundaryless Information Flow (KLP IIIRM.1-2)

D.13 TOGAF Certification Program

UNIT 13	TOGAF Certification Program
Purpose	The purpose of this Learning Unit is to help the Candidate understand the TOGAF Certification Program.
KLP Reference	None.
Learning Outcome	The Candidate must be able to: 1. Explain the TOGAF Certification Program, and distinguish between the levels for certification

Index

Printed in Great Britain
by Amazon